The EXTREME Searcher's Guide to
WEB SEARCH ENGINES

The EXTREME Searcher's Guide to
WEB SEARCH ENGINES

A Handbook for the Serious Searcher

Randolph Hock

Foreword by Paula Berinstein

CyberAge Books

The Extreme Searcher's Guide
to Web Search Engines:
A Handbook for the Serious Searcher

Library of Congress Cataloging-in-Publication Data

Hock, Randolph, 1944-
    The extreme searcher's guide to Web search engines : a handbook for the serious searcher / Randolph Hock ; foreword by Paula Berinstein.
        p.   cm.
    Includes index.
    ISBN: 0-910965-38-2 (hardcover)   ISBN: 0-910965-26-9
(pbk.)
      1. Web search engines.   I. Title.   II. Title: Web search engines.
    ZA4226.H63 1998
    025.04--dc21   98-46310
                                                       CIP

Printed and bound in the United States of America.
Cover design: Jacqueline Walter
Book Design: Patricia F. Kirkbride
Copy Editor: Diane Zelley
Indexer: Sharon Hughes
Managing Editor: Dorothy J. Pike

DEDICATION
To Pamela, Matthew, Stephen, and Elizabeth

TABLE OF CONTENTS

iLLUSTRATiONS

LiST oF TABLES

FOREWORD

One of the pleasures of reading mysteries is probing the minds of the detectives that inhabit them. How do these great men and women think? Along what paths do they reason, and in what whirring of that inner machinery does their genius lie? We devoted fans never tire of asking, "How did Holmes/Wimsey/Poirot figure that out?"

Search engines are the detectives of the Web, gathering and evaluating clues, attempting to eliminate red herrings, and zeroing in on whodunit—er, the answer. These cybertecs possess personalities as diverse and mysterious as their famous fictional counterparts and techniques as varied and inscrutable to the observer.

Fortunately for us, Ran Hock is no ordinary observer. In the elegant book you are holding, this teacher-cum-investigator performs some fancy detective work of his own to probe behind the facades of these virtual sleuths. You think you know the search engines? Yes, they're familiar, but even if you're a serious and longtime searcher, you may still be surprised by the tricks and manners of these characters. Hock uncovers them for you, revealing personalities and methods that resemble, in turn, Sherlock Holmes (pure logic), Nancy Drew (popular, smart, but a little amateurish), Lieutenant Columbo (his bewildered manner belies a keen intelligence), and yes, Inspector Clouseau, that bumbling imbecile whose successes are invariably a matter of dumb luck.

But this book is no theoretical exercise or mere character study. It's a practical how-to for those of us who don't have time to flail. It's even a book for those of us who assiduously read documentation, for Web search engine documentation can mislead woefully. Whether you've tinkered with strategies and syntax, tried every feature on the engine's home page, or conducted your own benchmarking, there's something here for you.

In this "dossier," Hock covers the following:

- What to expect—realistically—from Web search engines, and why

- What not to expect from these freelance techs (yes, they all have their vices)
- How search engines are constructed and work, in general (I think our author tailed them and took covert photos to get this information)
- Tips for effective searching, and how to use search engine features, like truncation, proximity, field searching, etc. (With this input from you, your hired gumshoe can solve the crime *tout de suite*.)
- Side-by-side comparisons of features and search results for the engines covered in the book
- An in-depth examination of each engine, its strengths, weaknesses, and quirks, with examples diverse enough to appeal to just about everyone (and which reveal the delightful depth and breadth of our author's interests)
- Informative screenshots you can actually read!

As you read this book, it will be easy to picture our author hunched over his computer for hours, conducting test after test, yelling "Aha!" as he finds documentation lies and errors, and painstakingly compiling his wisdom for you and me. If you see him at a conference, be sure to thank him. He'll be the one in the trench coat.

Paula Berinstein

Paula Berinstein is a professional researcher and author of several books, including Finding Statistics Online, Finding Images Online, *and* Communicating with Library Users. *As the founder of her own firm, Berinstein Research, she has specialized in researching exotic topics for the entertainment industry, businesses, and individuals since 1987. Prior to that, she was a programmer/systems analyst for the company that makes the space shuttle main engine, and also a reference librarian. She now writes full time and, in addition to books for information users, is a regular contributor to information industry publications, including* Searcher: The Magazine for Database Professionals, Online, *and* Database.

ACKNOWLEDGMENTS

Thanks to Tom Hogan for agreeing to publish this book and to my editor, John Bryans, who led me knowledgeably but gently through the process of turning the text into a book and some initially cryptic statements into something more readable. Any remaining rough spots are my fault, not his. Some credit for the title of the book should go to my friends in the New England Online Users Group (NENON), who first suggested "Extreme Searching" as a title for one of my seminars on search engines. Thanks also to the numerous students from my courses who recommended that I publish such a book. I now expect them to buy numerous copies.

iNTRoDUCTioN

"Fairy Tales Can Come True, It Can Happen to You"

Be careful what you wish for, you might get it. Over the years, and with varying degrees of seriousness, many people have wished for immediate publishing and worldwide distribution of anything anyone might want to write about, and immediate access to those and to other tens and tens of millions of documents. We got it. What do we do with it? Way back when the wish started becoming true (a couple of years ago when there were only a matter of millions of documents on the Web), we already realized the downside. We had the documents out there on the Web, but they were in unorganized piles in data "storage sheds" around the world instead of on nicely arranged shelves in well-cataloged libraries. To the rescue came Web search engines, then more search engines, then more search engines. Literally more search engines than most of us know what to do with.

Dealing effectively with this new situation, these new tools and the new and very different challenges is where the "extreme searcher" comes in—the searcher who wants and needs more than the ordinary—the serious searcher who won't or can't settle for run-of-the-mill results—the searcher who is willing to try something different and push the envelope. To be an extreme searcher requires neither extensive training nor extraordinary skills. What it does require is an understanding of the terrain and the equipment.

Which is where this book comes in. On the Web we have, for our searching pleasure, access to eight or so "major" search engines all promising simplicity of use and extraordinary retrieval power. Just how simple they are to use and how extraordinary the retrieval really is depend on one's particular needs at a particular moment. Just as the venerable *Readers' Guide* usually well serves the needs of the eighth-grade paper writer or the homeowner who needs help with a wet basement, so do these search engines provide simplicity of access for fairly simple questions. For the "serious" researcher, for whom this book is written, simplicity unfortunately also breeds the problem of lack of precision and sometimes missing the really good document. The goal of this book is to help the researcher achieve acceptable search results in terms of being able to find an adequate number of appropriately relevant documents.

The Extreme Searcher's Guide to Web Search Engines is intended as a practical resource for the "serious searcher." The book is "practical" in presenting material that will be useful in real searching situations. This includes "background" material to the degree to which that material can help the searcher understand what can and cannot be retrieved, and why some items are retrieved while others may be missed. Minute details about search engines that did not seem to contribute to that end are not included.

Serious searchers are defined here as those persons who can make frequent use of material from the Web for business or research purposes. Generally speaking, these users need greater retrieval capabilities than can be realized by using the simplest versions and approaches offered by search engine producers. Even a cursory examination confirms that the search engines aim for (as Infoseek describes them) "the average, non-technical consumer." Though the "average" search engine user may be able to get by with the simplest approach, there actually is much more retrieval power built into the various search engines— retrieval power that the serious searcher can and should capitalize on.

This book aims to facilitate more effective and efficient use of Web search engines by helping the reader :

- Learn the basic structure of the major search engines
- Become acquainted with the commonalities and differences between search engines
- Understand the main strengths and weaknesses of the major search engines
- Learn about and use the variety of options and features provided by search engines
- Pick up some tips and tricks that make searching more effective

These aims are addressed in a somewhat generalized manner in Chapter One: "Search Engines In General." Chapters Two through Ten include profiles of each of the major engines and some of the meta-search services. These profiles provide an overview of what each engine offers, and demonstrate how users can get the best performance from each engine.

Before moving on to some of the details, it may be important to address the issue of what is and what is not a Web search engine. For the purposes of this book, a Web search engine is a service provided through the World Wide Web that allows a user to enter a term or a combination of terms in order to locate Web pages of interest (note that the terms "search engines" and "search services" are used somewhat interchangeably). Muddying the picture somewhat is the recent introduction of the term "portal." Many of the search engine services are now positioning themselves, to varying degrees, as "Web portals"— primary gateways by which people enter the Web, starting points for getting what one needs from the Web. In doing so, these services have added a variety of features to attract users to their sites—including directories, free email, chat rooms, etc. The "search" function, though in many cases still central, is now one of several useful services they provide. In this book, the emphasis is on the search engine function, and the other services will be treated as "add-ons." The add-ons will be given some attention, since they are useful to the serious searcher, but the emphasis here will be on the services' capabilities for searching large portions of the overall Web.

Web search engines can either be general, attempting to cover the broad range of Web sites and pages, or they can be specialized, covering a specific subset of Web information. The term "search engine" can also be used to apply to those services or systems that allow searching of a specific database, such as MEDLINE, or a collection of databases. There are also an increasing number of search engines that cover a specific country or geographic region. These specialized search engines will not be addressed here. A working knowledge of the major search engines will help you understand the more specialized ones because (1) some of the more specialized ones use retrieval engines produced by the major services, and (2) the general structure of features and searching is similar.

Web search engines are usually distinguished from Web directories. The latter are services that arrange Web content in a way that allows the user to "browse" through a subject hierarchy or alphabetical list in order to identify relevant sites. The distinction between the two types of "finding tools" is not always clear. Yahoo!, the largest and best known Web directory, is also often described as a Web search engine. You can browse through the hierarchy, or you can enter terms and have Yahoo! search for those terms. Even better, Yahoo! integrates the two functions by allowing the user to use the hierarchy to narrow the breadth, then to search within only that portion of the hierarchy. Several of the search engines we will look at have directories associated with them. Yahoo! is the only major finding tool that fully integrates both the searching and the directory functions. Directories associated with the other engines are for the most part rather separate options.

This book evolved from courses on search engines created and presented by my training and consulting firm, Online Strategies. Enough of my students suggested that the course manual be published as a book that it eventually began to make sense. My initial reticence stemmed from the fact that Web search engines were evolving, disappearing, and "morphing" rapidly, and it seemed risky to put in print information likely to become outdated quickly. However, two factors tipped the balance in favor of going ahead—a combination of the apparent demand for a clear, concise, easy-to-use manual, and recognition that though the outward appearance of the services change frequently, the actual searching functions change much less frequently.

I ask that you keep in mind, though, that changes in search engines are still occurring rapidly. New engines may have appeared by the time this ink is dry. New features are likely to have been added to some engines, and some engines may have dropped some features. To make the task of keeping up a little easier, I am providing a site, The Extreme Searcher's Web Page, that will post changes as they relate to the content of this book. The Extreme Searcher's Web Page (**www.onstrat.com/engines**) is not meant as a general-purpose "search engine news" site, but rather as an ongoing "addendum and corrections" page that includes references to specific pages and chapters of this book.

In spite of the inevitable changes in search engines, the chances are very good that what is included herein will remain valid long enough to make this book useful to a broad range of users. What is covered in the first section about the general structure of search engines and the algorithms behind them is not likely to change radically. The intent of the discussion of the individual engines is to give a picture brief enough to be quickly read, but extensive enough to help the reader take full advantage of the strengths and unique aspects of each engine.

Chapter One provides background and generalizations that apply to most if not all of the major search engines. The intent here is to present and convey information that will help the reader understand how to squeeze the most out of search engines as well as to understand why and how certain Web pages will (or will not be) retrieved. By presenting common aspects of search engines here, we avoid monotonous repetition in the engine-specific chapters that follow.

Chapters Two through Nine include profiles of eight leading search engines. These eight were chosen because of their size and their prominence and/or strength as research tools. Much more emphasis is given to "searching" features of the engines than to the numerous and varied "add-ons"(extra features that often are not very closely related to the main search function of an engine). The add-ons are described fairly briefly. The Web "directories" that are attached to many of the search engines are given a moderate amount of attention. Each profile is designed to allow the searcher to easily grasp what the engine has to offer and how to take advantage of it.

Most of the information presented here is from the online documentation for the various engines and hundreds of hours of testing, experimentation, and experience regarding what really happens during a Web search. Some of the information was provided by the search engine producers through other means, such as press releases and direct contact.

As you explore and use these search engines, keep in mind that they don't always deliver on their producers' claims, and they don't always perform the way an experienced, serious searcher would like them to. Facing these realities can result in a happier, healthier you. We have at our fingertips some wonderful, even amazing (but certainly not perfect) research tools, and the information these engines can help deliver to us is often truly astonishing.

Enjoy, and profit!

Ran Hock

ABOUT THE EXTREME SEARCHER'S WEB PAGE

WWW.ONSTRAT.COM/ENGINES

The World Wide Web is ever changing and shifting, and as the Web goes, so go the search engines designed to explore and reveal its riches.

At the Online Strategies Web site you will find updates to the material included in the book. This resource, *The Extreme Searcher's Web Page*, includes details of important changes in the Web search engines. The emphasis of what is included is on those changes that affect how searchers can most effectively utilize and get the highest quality results from search engines. Wherever possible and practical, the page features active links to the search engines and related Web pages.

The Extreme Searcher's Web Page is available to you as a valued reader of *The Extreme Searcher's Guide to Web Search Engines*.

To access *The Extreme Searcher's Web Page*, an Internet connection and Web browser are required. Go to: www.onstrat.com/engines

Enjoy your visit, and please send feedback by email to: rehock@onstrat.com

Disclaimer:
Neither publisher nor author make any claim as to the results that may be obtained through the use of *The Extreme Searcher's Web Page* or of any of the Internet resources it references or links to. Neither publisher nor author will be held liable for any results, or lack thereof, obtained by the use of this page or any of its links; for any third-party charges; or for any hardware, software, or other problems that may occur as a result of using it. *The Extreme Searcher's Web Page* is subject to change or discontinuation without notice at the discretion of the publisher and author.

Search Engines in General

A VERY BRIEF HISTORY

Web search engines have a very brief history, about half a decade, and this brief section is a very brief summary of that brief history.

Before there were Web search engines, there was chaos. If you wanted to find something on the Internet, you needed to know its exact address. The first really significant step out of that chaos and toward a degree of organization of Internet content was the development of "gophers," server-based collections of Internet addresses arranged in a menu format. (The term "gopher" comes from the mascot for the University of Minnesota, from where the first Internet "gopher" emerged.) Gophers were non-HTML-based and typically indexed not much more than file titles or very brief descriptions. Gophers begat Veronica (which searched all of "gopherspace") and Veronica begat Jughead, but by that time they had become less relevant than even the comic strip characters after which they were named and few people even got around to figuring out what Jughead was.

The gopher lineage was barely more than a couple of years old when it was overshadowed by the rapid development of the World Wide Web, which allowed exploitation of hyperlinks, full-text searching, graphical browsers, and other easy-to-use and highly interactive technology—and the development of Web search engines.

The first successful Web search engine to emerge was WebCrawler, which came from the University of Washington and made its public debut in April of 1994. Within a year three competitors were on the scene: Lycos, Infoseek, and OpenText. In late 1995, AltaVista and Excite appeared. Interestingly, most of the actual searching technology of use to the serious searcher today was already present in varying degrees in these earlier search engines, including features such as Boolean, truncation, etc. Unfortunately—and the impact of this continues into the present—none of the search engines took advantage of the heavy-duty searching technology and approaches found in online services such as Dialog and Lexis-Nexis. Neither did the search engines nor their cousins, the Web directories, take advantage of the extensive subject classification theory and practice of the last hundred or so years. These points are relevant in a very practical way in that the serious searcher must recognize that most Web search engines were and are developed for the more casual searcher, not for those who can take advantage of more sophisticated approaches and techniques.

HotBot came along in 1996 and Northern Light in 1997. HotBot brought a more sophisticated yet easy-to-use interface coupled with a very large database (by the end of 1997, it was the largest available but a year later was overtaken by AltaVista). Northern Light brought an integration of Web searching and searching of proprietary information.

Among the "early" search engines, Open Text was the first to bite the dust. By early 1998 it was no longer available. There will undoubtedly be more disappearances before the turn of the century and probably the appearance of at least one or two more major search engines. In the meantime, the changes within current engines continue, but these are largely either superficial interface updates or involve new "add-ons"—those features and services that are provided as part of the services but are not an integral part of the searching function. We can hope that the producers of these tools will work on enhancing search capabilities, but at the moment there is not much evidence to support that hope. Some producers (most especially AltaVista's) seem to show little concern in even making the engine do what they say it does.

As with the rest of the business world, search engine companies are extremely susceptible to fads. In 1996 and 1997, the fad was to make sure that your engine had an "advanced" version, regardless of whether the advanced version really did anything more sophisticated or whether the same things could not have been incorporated into the original engine version. 1998 brought the "personalization" fad, which if done right can provide real benefits—especially to the serious searcher. Search engine providers have also moved to add free email and free home pages to their list of add-ons. The current fad (which I think may last because it has real value for many consumers) is to provide a somewhat integrated collection of these add-ons and call it a "Web portal." Watch what one does and expect most of the rest to follow suit.

The best hope for the serious searcher in the next few years is that at least a couple of the search engines will identify the serious searcher as a viable market niche. The more serious searchers know about search engines, the more that is likely to happen. So, moving in that direction …

HOW SEARCH ENGINES ARE PUT TOGETHER

Since discussions of search engines naturally lead dangerously close to an automotive metaphor, we might as well give in and go with that metaphor briefly. A danger is that already some readers may be saying to themselves: "I don't care what's under the hood of my vehicle, I just want to know how to drive it." Quite honestly, this book is not intended for the "driver" who does not care to know how to check the oil. It is intended for the researcher who wants to know at least a little more than the basics, who cares about taking a few extra steps that may very significantly improve the performance of his or her searching.

A search engine can be considered to have four or so main functional parts: (1) the engine's "spiders," which go out and find Web sites and pages; (2) the indexing program, which indexes what the spiders find as well as sites that are directly submitted by Web page creators; (3) the "retrieval engine," the algorithm and associated programming, devices, etc., which, upon request, retrieve material from the index; and (4) the graphical interface, which gathers query data from the user to feed to the retrieval engine. There is in most cases a fifth component that needs to be addressed, the "add-ons." These are the added features found on search engines' home pages, such as Web directories, featured sites, and various other tools. With regard to directories, it is especially important to note the degree to which they are, or are not, integrated into the actual searching capabilities of a search engine.

Spiders

Spiders, or crawlers, are the programs that go out to the Web to (1) identify new sites that are to be added to the search engine and (2) identify sites already covered that have changed. Spiders gather information about the content of pages from sites and feed that information to the search engine's indexing mechanism. Much could be said about how this happens, but for the searcher just a few points are relevant and provide an understanding of why some engines find certain pages and other engines miss those pages, even when the page is in the second engine's database. For many engines, more popular sites (such as those that are visited frequently and those that have lots of links to them) are crawled more thoroughly and more frequently than less popular sites. Spiders can be programmed for *depth* or for *breadth*, or both. Those programmed for depth identify not only main sites but also the subsidiary pages to the main page, the subsidiary pages of those pages, etc. Spiders programmed for *breadth* of sites are typically concerned with finding more main sites, but not necessarily identifying all the subsidiary pages of a site. As search engines mature, and become even more competitive, there will be a tendency to see a greater melding of both depth and breadth.

As well as the sites identified by the spiders, a large number of sites added to search engines come from direct submissions by Web page publishers. If you examine any search engine's home page, you will probably find a link that allows you or anyone else to submit a page to the search engine. In most cases, pages submitted will indeed be added to the database. All or most search engine producers examine submitted pages for "spam" (in this context, dirty tricks for unfairly increasing chances of a page being retrieved) and may also apply other criteria, but the chances are very good that a submitted page will end up in the engine's database.

(*Author Note:* In this discussion we are using the words "site" and "page" somewhat interchangeably. Technically speaking, a "site," usually thought of as corresponding to a particular domain name, can have many pages—even thousands of pages. Spiders find both new sites and new pages within old sites. Likewise, individual pages, as well as sites, can be submitted to a search engine.)

The collection of information about sites that is gathered by these spiders, and information from submitted sites, when organized and then indexed, makes up a given search engine's database.

The Indexing Program and the Index

In terms of what pages are actually retrieved by a query, indexing can be even more critical than the spidering process. Some search engines claim to index all of the words from every page. The catch is what the engines choose to regard as a "word." Some have a list of "stop words" (small, common words that are considered insignificant enough to be ignored) that they don't index. Sometimes what they leave out are the obvious candidates such as articles and conjunctions. Some leave out other high frequency, but potentially valuable words such as "Web" and "Internet." Sometimes numerals are left out, making it difficult, for example, to search for "Troop 13."

Most engines index the "high value" fields such as the title and the URL. Metatags are usually indexed, but not always (Metatags are words, phrases, or sentences that are placed in a special section of the

HTML code as a way of describing the content of the page. Metatags are not displayed when you view a page, though you can view them if you wish by telling your browser to show the "**page source**"). Without much imagination, it is easy to see how useful the content of metatags is for information retrieval. However, one engine, Excite, purposely has not indexed some metatags: the rather paternalistic excuse was that it is "protecting" users since metatags can be abused by Web page developers in order to get their page a higher "score" in search engine algorithms. (This caution was taken by Excite in spite of the fact that most engines have automatic, reasonably effective ways of dealing with such abuses. Excite's philosophy on this point was obviously not formulated with the serious searcher in mind.)

Those familiar with HTML know that frames are used in a large number of sites. (Frames are an HTML device that treats different parts of a page as somewhat independent "windows.") Some search engines do not index frames, thereby causing the possible loss to the searcher of some, even many relevant sites. This weakness is somewhat compensated for by the fact that the astute Web page developer will create a "no frames" version of their frame site in addition to the frames version.

Some search engines index the words in hypertext anchors and links (e.g., "**Click Here**"), names of Java "applets," links within image maps, etc. Other search engines do not. Understanding that there are these variations in indexing policy goes a long way toward explaining why relevant pages, even when in the search engine's database, may not be retrieved by some searches.

The Retrieval Engine

The retrieval engine is the program that receives your query and subsequently searches an engine's database to identify and deliver to you records that match your query. In effect, two major things happen as part of this process: The retrieval engine identifies the matching records by means of a "retrieval algorithm," and the engine then arranges the retrieved items in a particular order to be displayed to the user. These may happen more or less simultaneously, or they can be fairly distinct operations.

Retrieval algorithms are discussed in some detail later on. For the moment, we will just say that these programs utilize matching criteria to determine which records contain particular words, phrases, and combinations of same. They may also match other user-specified criteria such as whether a particular page contains audio or image files.

The part of the search engine that estimates relevance of records may be closely integrated into the retrieval algorithm or it may be a separate process. Even when it is a fairly separate process, the separateness may not be obvious to the user, and usually does not need to be.

The HTML Interface

What the users see when they connect with a search engine is the HTML (HyperText Markup Language)-based interface. This interface gathers query data from the user and sends that data to the search engine for retrieval. Its most obvious function is to provide a means for the user to specify the query. However the interface also serves several other functions, including providing a space for advertisers (and consequently generating revenue for the search engine company), providing links to add-ons (see below), and providing links to "Help" pages and other information.

Add-Ons

What are discussed as "add-ons" are those additional features that appear on the service's interface that are not a part of the searching function. For our present purposes, we will define "searching" as the process in which a user enters specific criteria and the service searches a database to identify and return Web pages that match the criteria. This is distinguished from "browsing," where, without entering any specific criteria, the user can scan an organized listing (alphabetic or classified), often going through a series of layers or levels to identify items of interest. Directories are browsed, search engines and databases are searched. An argument could easily be made that "add-ons" is not the best term for what is discussed here, that these features are an integral part of these services, not just something "added on." The term will be used anyway, since for the serious searcher the main utility of the services are their searching capabilities. Added services (directories, for example) are often found in better form, with more extensive content, elsewhere on the Web.

It should be pointed out that there are special cases, most outstandingly Yahoo!, in which the searching function and the directory functions are integrated. Yahoo! is more often though of as a directory than as a database, but because of the degree of integration of the two functions it deserves a seat in both camps. (The people at Yahoo! are emphatic that their product is a "directory" rather than a "search engine.") Yahoo! integrates browsing particularly well because, when "searching," Yahoo!'s classification headings are searched, and when "browsing" at any of the levels within the classification scheme, the searcher can choose to apply search criteria to the pages within that classification level. Other engines also have directories that can be searched, but with a lesser degree of integration than with Yahoo!.

In addition to directories, add-ons can include links to other searchable databases such as news databases, links to specific sites such as MapQuest, sites for stock market information, links to chat rooms, etc.

In the chapters on the individual services that follow, add-ons will be identified and discussed to varying degrees—depending upon how integrated they are with the searching function, or how unique and interesting an add-on is. An attempt is made by means of the index at the back of the book to provide a way for you to easily identify which engines have a particular add-on or type of add-on.

COMPONENTS OF A TYPICAL SEARCH ENGINE HOME PAGE

The visual appearance of the home pages for the various search engine services differs tremendously. This is actually somewhat beneficial to searchers as a way of helping them maintain a mental image of each of the various services. However, until one has gotten fairly intimate with several engines, the lack of consistency can create confusion. For this reason, it will be worthwhile to look at a "typical" search engine service home page to identify the content and features the services tend to have in common. Once the commonality is seen, the easier will be to take a quick look at any search engine service and get a feel for what can be done with it.

HotBot contains most of the elements typically found on search engine home pages. See Figure 1.1 below.

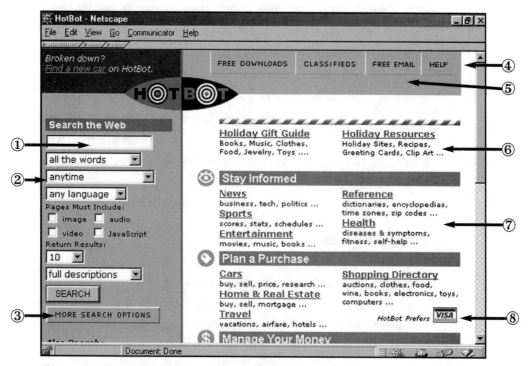

Figure 1.1　Typical Web Search Engine home page (HotBot)

① Query Box	⑤ Add-ons
② Search Options	⑥ Site Promotion
③ Link to Advanced search mode	⑦ Directory/channels
④ Help link	⑧ Advertisement

Search Options

Most search engines provide a choice as to what collection of sources is to be searched. In some cases the choice may be to search either all of the engine's Web database or a portion of it. In other cases the options may include searches of other collections (databases), such as Usenet postings.

The most obvious choice is "the Web," meaning all of the Web pages included within the database of a given search service. Often, a text box or radio buttons are provided for search options. When this is the case, alternatives offered are usually ones for which searchability features are basically the same as for the Web search.

Frequently, there will be links elsewhere on the page for searching other databases (such as stock information databases), but for these links the search engine used is usually different, sometimes provided by another company. For example, HotBot provides links for searching Usenet, news, stocks, and other databases. For some of these, the search interface looks more or less similar to the main HotBot interface, but for others, the look and options are quite different. With the stocks link, not surprisingly, the only search options are by ticker symbol or company name. The Usenet search is powered by Deja News with very different search options.

Query Boxes

Query boxes, which in some cases are the only boxes, are the heart of it all. It is here where you enter your query. Exactly what you can enter (phrases, Boolean logic, etc.) depends upon the search engine. (Boolean logic, in this context, is the capability of using "operators" such as AND, OR, and NOT to retrieve only those records that include a particular combination of terms.)

Link to the Advanced Version

For all engines that provide an advanced version option, there will be a link somewhere on the home page that leads to the more advanced version. Often the link itself is surprisingly small, almost as if they really don't want you to see it. Keep in mind that if you prefer the advanced version, which most serious searchers will (for most engines), you can just bookmark the advanced version's page rather than, or in addition to, the service's main home page.

Advertising

Advertising on search engines is almost inevitable. For most companies that provide these search engines, advertising and licensing of their software provide the main revenue stream from search engine operations.

Directory (Topics, Channels, Classification)

For the major engines, listings of additional Web information resources usually appear in one of the following formats (or as a variation on one of the following):

- A "directory," or classified list of selected sites. Note that these selected sites constitute only a small portion of the sites found in a given search engine's database.
- Links to "channels," or specialized pages relevant to broad topics like "business," "entertainment," or "sports." Each of these pages may contain links, searchable sites, etc.

In some cases, as with Infoseek and Yahoo!, after choosing one of these categories you can opt to search strictly within the sites listed for that category.

Site Promotion

Each search engine producer (not unexpectedly) seems compelled to put in a plug for how great their search service is, usually by highlighting special features or content.

Add-Ons

In addition to directories, the home page may provide additional links to sites of interest, and other bonus features.

Help Links

Help links will lead you to one or more pages that explain how the search engine allegedly works. While most of what you read in the help pages will be correct, unfortunately some services promise things they do not deliver. In some cases they provide features that are not documented in the help screens. Some services have been known to make major changes without taking the time to update their help screens.

Learn two or three engines well, but use the others frequently.

WHAT TO REALISTICALLY EXPECT FROM WEB SEARCH ENGINES

Especially for those who have extensively searched such online services as Dialog and Lexis-Nexis, expectations for Web search engines will need to be tempered considerably. The variety of features, sophistication, and reliability of features, as well as reliability of retrieval provided by Web search engines is often primitive compared to those established commercial services. Dialog and Nexis would be mobbed by hordes of pitchfork-wielding users if they were to suddenly begin providing the low level of reliability, sophistication, and customer support currently provided in some cases by some of the search engines.

On the other hand, the level of tolerance of such shortcomings can be significantly raised when we remind ourselves that the Web search services are free. There are no per-minute charges, no sub-scription charges, and no output charges.

The gap between traditional retrieval expectations and Web search expectations is further narrowed when a couple of other factors are considered. Recognition of both of these factors is important for the searcher who wants to get the most out of either kind of search service.

First, Web search engines are dealing with very unstructured data, or at least data with very little consistency of structure. Indeed, there is a definite structure to the HTML behind the Web pages, but for the actual intellectual content, about the only "intellectual" structure is found in the titles and metatags. The body of the pages has little consistent structure that the Web search service can use for structured searching.

Second, the sheer volume of data currently on the Web in combination with the volume added every day should add a degree of respect for what the Web search engines have accomplished in a very short period of time. The fact that there is at least an elementary level of access to the multiple million pages of material is a feat that should inspire much more awe than disappointment.

In a recent article, "Searching the World Wide Web" (Science 280:98-100, 1998), S. R. Lawrence and C. L. Giles reported on an extensive study of the degree to which search engines cover the total content of the Web. In the study, the researchers estimated that the Web contains 320 million pages of information and that the major search engines cover well less than half of that material. They estimated that of the 320 million pages, HotBot only covers 34%, AltaVista 28%, Northern Light 20%, Excite 14%, Infoseek 10%, and Lycos 3%.

To add some perspective to those numbers, keep in mind that covering a third or so of the published Web pages may actually be pretty good. Though there are of course the big issues of selectivity and quality to consider, in regard to extent of coverage keep in mind that more traditional indexing services have never covered anywhere near those kinds of percentages of "published" material. Respected services such as *Chemical Abstracts*, *Psychological Abstracts*, and others do not even make an attempt to cover everything published that makes mention of, respectively, chemistry or psychology. Take advantage of what the Web search engines do cover, and search more than one engine when you want to retrieve as much on your topic as possible.

For a reasonable set of expectations regarding searchability, there is one overreaching aspect that needs to be considered. In general, most search engines are not designed for the *serious searcher*. For the most part, they are designed for the casual user, not the person who needs to apply what they retrieve in the business and research environment. When a search engine's documentation uses *Baywatch* stars in its search examples, we get a sense of its assumed audience. Facing this fact while at the same time making the best use of what is offered can prove to be the prudent approach. If serious users take advantage of the more sophisticated features offered, more sophisticated features may follow. With the number of competing search engines catering to the casual searcher, one or two may break away and target those who need heavier-duty retrieval power.

There are some other things NOT to expect:

- Consistency from one search engine to another
- The traditional tools you are used to with the older online vendors (controlled vocabulary, full range of Boolean and proximity connectors, choice of formats, etc.)
- Bibliographic searching. For listings of what has been published in journals, books, technical reports, dissertations, etc., most Web search engines generally will not be useful. The best bet here is to either use one of the commercial services or find a database on the Web, such as Medline, that covers your area of interest.
- To know what is happening during the search. Experienced online researchers often like to know all the finer details of what is happening behind the scenes so that they can have a good sense of whether they are really accomplishing their retrieval goals. With the small level of detail provided by

Web search engines, in combination with some obvious inconsistencies, extensive knowledge of the details is at present not achievable.

Finally, do *not* expect all the specifics you learn about any specific search engine today to be true tomorrow. Rather, learn what factors are involved in the searching process so you can interpret what you are seeing and so you can make the next move in a reasoned manner.

SUBJECT MATTER COVERED BY SEARCH ENGINES

For none of the search engines covered here is there any documented intent to focus on one type of Web page subject content over another. Experience also confirms this lack of intent. For many add-ons there is an obvious slant, more or less, toward consumer vs. professional research information.

Bookmark your favorite search engines for direct access, rather than using the search links offered through your Web browser (for instance, the "Net Search" page on Netscape, and the "Search" page on Internet Explorer).

UPDATE FREQUENCY

The "currentness" of the contents of a Web search service's database is dependent upon how frequently spiders crawl known sites, how quickly the new and changed pages they find are added to the database, and how quickly "submitted URLs" are visited and added to the database.

Even within a single Web search service, these factors can change frequently. Sites currently within a search engine's database may be revisited every few weeks, but more popular sites may be visited more frequently and less popular sites less frequently.

The time span from when a new page was submitted or crawled until it gets fully indexed has ranged from a day (maybe less) to a matter of months. Various engines make various claims, with varying levels of credibility. You may be able to find a page that was added yesterday. However, be aware that it may also take weeks or months in some engines. Pages that are linked from high profile sites have a good chance of being found more quickly than those from obscure sites.

Some services promise to get submitted sites added within a day or two, while others let you know it may be a matter of weeks. Those that promise "within a few minutes" most likely will only get the URL added within that time, not the indexed contents of the page.

Also, just because a page has been added to the database does not mean that it is fully indexed. This may be done in stages, with the URL itself indexed first, then the title and—maybe even months later—the text of the page.

TYPICAL RETRIEVAL AND RANKING FACTORS

Once users enter their query, that input goes to the program that searches the engine's database to determine (1) which records should be considered as having matched the query, and (2) in what order those records should be displayed. These two functions can work rather independently or they can be essentially a single function.

The first function, the identification of records, is most typically done based on either (a) using a default approach in which the user has entered terms, phrases, or sentences without any required syntax, or (b) using input from the user that conforms to a syntax involving criteria such as Boolean operators, proximity operators, field specifiers, etc.

When the user has not used a structured syntax, the most simplistic approach for identifying the records is for the retrieval program to take all or some of the words the user entered, connect them with either a Boolean AND or OR and search the database using that Boolean expression. With only a small degree of marketing license, this can be referred to as "natural language searching"—which in a rudimentary sense it is. The people who have spent a major portion of their lives working with the tremendously sophisticated and complicated aspects of natural language processing (NLP) may be understandably annoyed when natural language terminology is used so loosely. Most search engines go beyond that rudimentary form and indeed make use of more sophisticated approaches and techniques. In most of the major engines, however, whether explicitly or otherwise, the Boolean matching is an integral part of the whole process. There are alternatives, however, that bypass the Boolean and identify the records to be retrieved on the basis of more sophisticated linguistic analysis involving such factors as co-occurrence of terms.

When the user makes use of a specified syntax, such as Boolean, it usually (but not always) overrides an engine's default algorithm. By choosing to go with a syntax, the user is saying, "Thanks anyway, but I know what I'm doing and I'd prefer to take more control of the process." Some might think of the two approaches as the difference between a TV dinner and a meal prepared from scratch. The relative merits of the product depend on how good a cook one is. (Taking this metaphor just a bit further, how good a cook does one have to be to do better than a TV dinner?)

A single engine may provide all of these alternatives—a default algorithm based on implicit Boolean and other criteria, user-applied syntax, and sophisticated linguistic analysis.

With the first function of the program being the identification of "qualifying" records, the second major function of the search engine's retrieval/ranking program is to determine the relative relevance of each record. This is often expressed as a "score" or "ranking," i.e., the program's estimate as to how well a particular record meets the intent of the query. As stated above, this can be integrated into the first function, with a record's "ranking" determining whether or not the record is retrieved.

Because of the competitive nature of the search engine business, details of the retrieval and ranking algorithms are closely guarded. For effective use of search engines, it is useful to go into a little more detail as to the kinds of factors that are involved: the things the search engine looks for in a record to determine if it should be retrieved and how it should be ranked in terms of relevance. The latter usually determines the order in which records are presented to the user. In the profiles later in this book, the "known" factors for each engine will be discussed briefly. Those interested in knowing more should examine whatever details are provided in a given engine's online documentation.

The factors that go into determining whether or not the record is retrieved and the record's ranking (score) usually incorporate some combination of the following:

- Frequency of terms
- Number of terms in the query that are matched
- Weighting by field (e.g., Title counts more than summary)
- Proximity of terms
- Word variants (and/or truncation)
- Case sensitivity
- Occurrence of terms in a classification scheme vs. just in the document
- When a term is found in the classification hierarchy, the level in the hierarchy
- Analysis of documents in the database (term association, associative networks, cluster analysis, co-occurrence, etc.)
- Weighting according to the order in which the searcher entered terms
- Relevance feedback ("Find more like this") applied to retrieved records

If it's not documented, "guess" but don't "assume." If it *is* documented, don't necessarily believe it.

THE BIG QUESTION: RELEVANCE RANKING OR BOOLEAN LOGIC?

Perhaps the biggest question facing the searcher is whether to take advantage of a search engine's default searching mode or to use Boolean Logic and other features to take fuller personal control of the retrieval—in other words, whether to let the search engine's relevance ranking algorithm decide on which Web pages are relevant, or to use one's own searching skills, knowledge of language, and knowledge of the subject to more precisely identify the needed records.

The answers is: It depends. It depends primarily on the nature of the question, and on the searcher's skills.

First, the nature of the question. If the question is rather general and you expect that there will be a lot more relevant material on the Web than you actually need, then this is a good opportunity to let the search engine do its thing. Put in a list of terms describing your topic and let the engine have at it. For other questions, it never hurts to just go ahead and try it out in the default mode. The most you will lose is two or three minutes and the kinds of records you see retrieved may help you formulate your own Boolean or other query.

Second, the searcher's skills. Every serious searcher should know Boolean well enough to use it effectively. Serious searchers should also have an appreciation of the benefits of field searching and proximity options and know how to use them. The less these skills are present, the more the searcher will need to rely on the search engine's default mode. If a searcher is not adept at the use of these features, they should make use of the pull-down windows (or other devices) that many engines make available in order to achieve the effects of Boolean, field searching, etc.

If you do decide to use the default algorithm, I recommend you do the following:

- Enter the words that describe your topic with the more critical ones listed first. Some search engines give more weight to the words you list first.
- If one or more concepts in your topic has possible synonyms or alternate terms, enter those as well—but not too many of them. Too many synonyms can slant the retrieval and cause your other concept(s) to receive too little attention. If you are doing a search on the Argentinean cattle industry, you might try: **Argentina Argentinean cattle beef industry business**
- If you do not get good results, try rearranging the order of words.
- If the search engine allows it, use the **+word** option (discussed later in this chapter, in the section on Boolean) to insist that a word be present. For example: **+Argentina cattle beef industry** (Note that, typically, the **+word** option will not override and disable the relevance ranking algorithm as **AND, OR,** and **NOT** will). Likewise, if you want to insist that a word not be present, and the engine allows it, use the **-word** option.
- If the first few pages of results do not give you what you are looking for, either try another engine or give up, for the moment, on the relevance ranking and make use of Boolean, field searching, proximity, etc., to take personal control of the process.

It would be nice to be able to provide clear-cut, foolproof rules for when to use the default mode and when to employ Boolean and other search techniques. Unfortunately, there are too many variables to be able to do so. Perhaps the closest to a set of basic rules is this:

- Be willing to try each approach (default relevance ranking, Boolean)

- If one approach doesn't work, try another
- Know the options (advanced features) that are available to you

If you don't easily find what you are looking for in one engine, try another. A corollary to this (which you'll hear again) is this: In searches where you need to be exhaustive, or when you are looking for the best answer among several possible answers, search more than one search engine.

TYPICAL ADVANCED SEARCH OPTIONS

Features typically offered by Web search engines include options to search only selected portions of the database, Boolean logic, truncation, phrase searching, proximity searching, proper name searching, and field searching, plus choice of output format and number of records to appear on each results page.

Selection of What Is to Be Searched

When using search engines that have an accompanying directory, you may be given a choice as to whether to search the entire database or just the sites that are included in the directory. With Northern Light, for instance, you're given the option of searching Web documents, Northern Light's collection of proprietary documents, or both. You may also be given choices of searching Usenet, email directories, or other options.

When you choose to search an area other than "the Web," you will in many cases be transferring to an interface that is significantly different from the interface for searching the Web. The search engine service may attempt to make such an interface look like its own as much as possible, but because of differences in the types of information covered, it may out of necessity look quite different.

Boolean

Boolean (or Boolean logic, or Boolean algebra, etc.), for our purposes here, can be described as the use of operators such as AND, OR, and NOT to identify those pages (records) that contain a specific combination of terms.

If an engine has full Boolean capabilities, it will offer the following search options or the equivalents of each:

AND—to specify that both words must be present. For instance:

> automobile AND sales

would retrieve only those pages where both the word "automobile" and the word "sales" are present on the same page (same record).

OR—to specify that either word can be present. For instance:

> automobile OR car

would retrieve all of those pages (records) that have the word "automobile" plus all of those pages (records) that have the word "car."

NOT—to exclude a word. For instance:

> automobile NOT van

would retrieve all those pages (records) that have the word "automobile" except those that have the word "van." All those with "van" would be excluded.

Nesting Capabilities (using parentheses)

For instance:

> (automobile OR car) AND sales

would retrieve all the records that have the word "sales" and also have either the word "automobile" or "car." Note that the same effect would not necessarily result if the parentheses are omitted.

Several engines have partial Boolean search capabilities, offering one or more but not all of the above options (often AND in the form of +word, and NOT in the form of -word). The most commonly missing feature is the nesting capability. Without this capability, complex Boolean queries—especially those involving groupings of OR terms—cannot be accomplished.

A typical expression using the full range of Boolean functions would be:

"chemical industry" AND (Mexico OR Mexican) NOT pollution

Table 1.1 (see below) illustrates how the above search phrase would be expressed or approximated in each of the major search engines (for engines with more than one version, the version shown is the one that provides the greatest Boolean capability).

Be aware that use of Boolean operators in the form of AND, OR, NOT and BUT NOT will usually override an engine's built-in relevance retrieval, while -word and +word usually will not.

Table 1.1 Comparison of Boolean Statements in Different Search Engines

Search Engine	Full Boolean?	Expression
AltaVista (Advanced)	yes	"chemical industry" AND (Mexico OR Mexican) AND NOT pollution
Excite (Basic)	yes	"chemical industry" AND (Mexico OR Mexican) AND NOT pollution
HotBot	yes	"chemical industry" AND (Mexico OR Mexican) NOT pollution
Infoseek	no	+"chemical industry" +Mexico
Lycos Pro Search	yes	"chemical industry" AND (Mexico OR Mexican) NOT pollution
Northern Light	yes	"chemical industry" AND (Mexico OR Mexican) NOT pollution
WebCrawler	yes	"chemical industry" AND (Mexico OR Mexican) NOT pollution
Yahoo!	no	+"chemical industry" +Mexic*[asterisk is for truncating for "Mexico" or "Mexican." See below.]

If you are in a hurry and don't want to bother checking to see if the search engine you are using offers Boolean searching, go ahead and use AND, OR and NOT. If the engine doesn't apply them, chances are it will ignore these words.

Truncation

Truncation, the facility for searching on the stem or root of a word or allowing for variable characters, is a feature available in some of the search engines. It can either be user-controlled or automatic. You will often see this feature referred to as "wildcards."

Table 1.2 Truncation Features in Different Search Engines

Engine	Automatic or User-Controlled	Truncation Symbol	Example(s)	Special Notes
AltaVista	User-Controlled	*	horse* lab*r	Min. 3 char. Will match from 0-5 lower case additional char. Internal truncation allowed
Excite	Automatic		horse mouse	"Concept-based retrieval" approximates automatic truncation
HotBot	User-Controlled	*	horse*	Also provides an automatic stemming option
Infoseek	Automatic	*(for endings)	horse mouse	Also retrieves common variants, such as mice when mouse is searched
Northern Light	User-Controlled	%(for internal)	horse* workm%n	Minimum 5 leading characters.
Yahoo!	User-Controlled	*	manufact*	Some automatic truncation also takes place

Phrase and Proximity Searching

Search engines may allow the user to specify how close two words should be to each other. This may take the form of "phrase searching" where a precise phrase of two or more words can be entered and that exact phrase searched. This is most commonly accomplished by entering the phrase with double quotation marks around it. Some services allow additional flexibility with the NEAR or similar operators.

The NEAR operator may allow for two words to be a certain distance apart, sometimes allowing the searcher to specify the maximum distance. In Lycos Pro Search, for example:

medical NEAR/5 malpractice

would find records that contain both words no further than five words apart.

The NEAR operator is an excellent way to get high precision while allowing for a number of ways in which a writer may address a concept. In some cases, the searcher can specify whether the words need to be in a specific order, or if either word may come first. Other variations on this theme may also be provided. See the Search Engines Features Guide, Table 1.5 (beginning on page 40), and the individual search engine profiles for details.

Name Searching

The ability to search specifically for names of companies and people is something that some search engines can accomplish "approximately" by virtue of an ability to distinguish between upper and lower case characters. When these engines receive a query in which the first letters of the words are capitalized, they assume it may be a proper name.

The engines have no magical way of knowing whether what you enter is indeed a "name." In HotBot for example, when specifying a search for "the person," HotBot found over 3,000 pages with the alleged "person" named "Frank Discussion." (Frank: If you are really out there, my sincerest apologies for doubting your existence. I hope it will cause no long-lasting identity crisis.)

Name Searching Tips

- Capitalize names appropriately, so you can copy and paste the name effectively from one engine to another
- Use the NEAR operator when available (AltaVista-Advanced, and Lycos Pro Search), and when possible, use NEAR/2 (Lycos Pro Search). This will allow for the name to be inverted and will also allow for middle names. For example, in Lycos Pro Search:

    George NEAR/2 Bush

  will retrieve:

    George Bush
    George Herbert Walker Bush
    Bush, George

- If an engine doesn't have the NEAR operator:
    1. Put the name in double quotes " "
    2. Enter all the possible variants ORed together
        Example: "Dwight Eisenhower" OR
                "Dwight David Eisenhower" OR
                "Dwight D Eisenhower" OR
                "Eisenhower, Dwight"

The above example will work in:

AltaVista—Advanced
HotBot (*choose "the Boolean phrase" in the "Look for" box.*)
Excite (*a number of irrelevant pages will also be retrieved*)
Lycos Pro Search (*choose the "any of the words" search choice*)
Northern Light

Note that because of the number of records on someone like Eisenhower, you will probably want to combine the name terms with further qualifications. Also, don't forget to take advantage of your computer's "copy and paste" capability to carry your query from engine to engine, instead of retyping the query each time.

Field Searching:
Searching Within Specific Parts of a Record

Compared to traditional online services (Dialog, Lexis/Nexis, etc.), field searching with Web search engines is fairly rudimentary. Most engines provide only a half-dozen or so searchable fields compared to twenty to over two hundred with "old-time" online services. Some engines provide no field searching capability at all.

Table 1.3 (see page 28) summarizes which fields are searchable in each engine, and how those fields are searched.

Image Searching Tips

AltaVista, HotBot, Infoseek, and Lycos all provide image searching capabilities. Whether you are looking for an image of a person, place, thing, or whatever, one of these engines can probably lead you to it.

- In **AltaVista**, click on the AV Photo Finder link and you are taken to a special database of images from the Web and from the Corbis collection of over a half-million images. A search results in a display of thumbnail versions of the images with options for viewing the full image. In your search you can specify photos, artwork, color, or black and white.
- With **Lycos**, click the "Pictures and Sounds" link on the home page, then browse the "Now & Then" image collection categories. You'll be taken to thumbnail images from which you can choose the larger image. Alternatively, if you choose the Web search option, your search will take you to records for images found on the Web and from there directly to the image. The "titles" of the records you retrieve are from the ALT tag in the HTML coding. The downside is that for many images on the Web, no ALT tag is assigned.
- In **Infoseek**, use the "alt:" prefix. For example, search for alt:paramecium. You'll be taken to pages that contain the word in the image's ALT tag.
- In **HotBot**, enter a query in the query box, then click the "image" checkbox under "Pages must include." HotBot will probably retrieve a lot of pages, but there is a good chance that only a few of them will contain the image you are seeking. What you are retrieving are all pages which mention your topic and also contain an image.

In Infoseek and HotBot, when you go to a page that is said to have a particular image, and you can't find it quickly, if you are using Netscape to to View - Page Info. You'll see a list of all the images, plus other information about the structure and content of the page.

For a very good look at the numerous aspects of online image searching, see Paula Berinstein's book, *Finding Images Online* (Information Today, Inc., Medford, NJ). Information is available at the author's Web site at **www.berinsteinresearch.com**

Table 1.3 Field Searching Using Different Search Engines

ENGINE	FIELD	SEARCHED FROM (1)	PREFIX/ SYNTAX	EXAMPLES
AltaVista	**Date**	Date range boxes	dd/mmm/yr	09/jan/97 to 10/oct/97
	Title	Query box	title:	title:"San Jose Mercury"
	URL			
	Domain	" "	domain:	domain:uk
	host	" "	host:	host:faxon.com
	URL	" "	url:	url:whale.simmons.edu
				url:whale.simmons
				url:simons.edu/archives
	anchor	" "	anchor:	anchor:contact
	applet	" "	applet:	applet:class
	image	" "	image:	image:reindeer
	link	" "	link:	link:adlittle
	object	" "	object:	object:marquee
	text	" "	text:	text:Marblehead
	language	Language window	(choose from list)	French
	Usenet			
	from	Query box	from:	from:ran@onstrat.com
	subject	" "	subject:	subject:"search engines"
	summary	" "	summary:	summary:problems
	newsgroup	" "	newsgroup:	newsgroup:asis
	keywords	" "	keywords:	keywords:conference
HotBot	***Using Window (Panel) Choices:***			
	date	Date window	(choose from list)	*In the last week* [Advanced version: <u>after</u> or <u>before</u> date selected from list]
	title	"Look for" box	(choose "the page title" then use text box)	ostrich
	URL			
	Domain	Location panel	(text box)	uk
	host	" "	" "	faxon.com
	URL	" "	" "	edu
				simmons.edu
				whale.simmons.edu
	continent	Location panel	(choose from list)	North America
				North America (.com)
	media type	Media type panel	(checkboxes)	Image
				Audio
	file extension	Media type panel	(text box)	.gif
	Using Prefixes			
	Date (2)			
	after	Query box	after:dd/mm/yy	after:8/6/97
	before	" "	before:	before:10/12/97

Table 1.3 Field Searching Using Different Search Engines *cont.*

ENGINE	FIELD	SEARCHED FROM (1)	PREFIX/ SYNTAX	EXAMPLES
HotBot *cont.*	*URL* **domain**	Query Box	domain:	domain:org domain:org domain:ipl.org domain:hypatia.ipl.org
	page depth	" "	depth:	depth:3
	link (domain)	" "	linkdomain	linkdomain:four11.com
	link (extension)	" "	linkext:	linkext:ra
	scriptlanguage	" "	scriptlanguage:	scriptlanguage:java
	newsgroup	" "	newsgroup:	newsgroup:asis-1
	feature	" "	feature:	feature:video feature:applet feature:image feature:audio
Infoseek	**title**	Query Box	title:	title:"search engine"
	URL **url**	" "	url:	url:whale:simmons url:whale.simmons.edu url:simmons.edu/archives
	site (host)	" "	site:	site:simmons.edu site:whale.simmons.edu
	link	" "	link:	link:ancestry.com
	images	" "	alt:	alt:truman
Lycos	**title**	Pro Search Page	(text box)	"search engines"
	URL	" " "	" "	ancestry.com
	sound	" " "	(choose from list)	roosevelt
	pictures	" " "	" " "	locomotives
Northern Light	*Home page version* **URL**	Query box	url:	url:whale:simmons url:whale:simmons.edu url:simmons.edu/archives
	title (3)	Query box	title:	title:field searching title:"online strategies"
	publication (4)(5)	Query box	pub:	pub:"Agricultural History"
	company	Query box	company:	company:"General Motors"
	ticker	Query box	ticker:	ticker:bur
	text (6)	Query box	text:	text:apparel
	industry	Industry Search page	(choose from list)	Healthcare
	Power Search version: **URL**	"Words in URL" box	(text box)	whale.simmons whale.simmons.edu simmons.edu/archives

Table 1.3   Field Searching Using Different Search Engines *cont.*

ENGINE	FIELD	SEARCHED FROM (1)	PREFIX/ SYNTAX	EXAMPLES
Northern Light *cont.*	**Power Search version:** **title** (3)	"Words in title" box	(text box)	"field searching" "online strategies"
	publication (4)(5)	"Publication name" box on Publication Search page"	(text box)	"Agricultural History"
	Industry	"Select Industry" checkboxes on Industry Search page	(checkboxes)	Food & Beverage
Yahoo	**title** **URL**	Query box " "	t: u:	t:"molecular magnetism" u:mapquest

(1) This column indicates where to look on the page or which version of the engine to use

(2) Using the date prefixes in HotBot does not seem to be working consistently

(3) In Northern Light, if multiple words are entered after the prefix, with no quotation marks, the search will retrieve those words anywhere in that field, not necessarily the specific phrase

(4) The pub, ticker, and company prefixes will only retrieve items from the Northern Light Special Collection

(5) Publication can also be searched from Northern Light's "Publication Search" page (click Publication Search tab on main page)

(6) If you are using other prefixes in a Boolean statement, you must specify the text prefix for those terms you want to search in the text of the page, e.g., URL:cornell AND text:hotel

Date Searching—Special Consideration

Be aware that within Web search engines, "date" usually does not refer to the date of publication of the content of a Web page, but rather to the date when the page was created or last modified. If no creation or "last modified" date is on the page, the engine may use the date the page was picked up or last visited by the search engine.

Output Options

In reporting an answer, most engines tell you how many records were retrieved. They may also give the counts for each individual term if the query contained more than one term.

Most engines provide either one, two, or three format options, the short one being just URL or title, a medium including a few other elements, and a more detailed format that includes a summary of the page or the first few words of the page, typically Title, URL, Summary, etc.

The engines typically display ten records per page as the default, with options for larger increments, in some cases up to 100 per page.

BENCHMARKS

To understand the differences between the search engines, it makes sense to do some specific head-to-head retrieval comparisons. In interpreting the results of such comparisons, considerable caution should be applied because of the numerous variables involved, such as presence of duplicates among the results in any engine, reliability of numbers reported by the engines, constant changes in sizes of the databases and so on. The best benchmarking for search engines is probably that done by an individual comparing results for words, phrases, etc. in subject areas relevant to the individual's particular area of research. The following "benchmarks" however, which come from a variety of fields, should give some idea of the relative performance of the engines.

Before examining the chart that follows (Table 1.4 on pages 32-33), the reader should acknowledge some caveats. First, the numbers shown are those *reported by the service* for each search. It is not feasible to check whether the numbers are actually "correct" in terms of whether each of the reported numbers represents a valid, unduplicated, still-available page.

Perhaps most importantly, because of the degree of overlap, or more particularly the low degree of overlap, there is one conclusion that should *not* be drawn from the chart: that one can pick the engine with consistently highest numbers and stick with that one engine. That conclusion would ignore the fact that each of the major engines can produce a significant number of results that are not found by its "competitors." This will be discussed in more

Table 1.4 Benchmarking Results

	AltaVista	Excite	HotBot	Infoseek
Aberystwyth	**30,020**	4,635	8,450	6,497
laparoscopy	**24,450**	2,610	4,510	4,093
Alvin Toffler	3,060	1,392	3,150	1,610
sidereal messenger	126	40	56	73
Crumpton AND Maryland	204	69	170	30
(trilobite OR trilobites) AND morphology	252	121	320	*
carolingian AND (monastery OR monasteries)	**610**	243	580	*

detail in the following section. Even the smaller engines often retrieve records not retrieved by the larger engines.

What *can* be concluded is that there is a wide variation in the retrieval of the various engines, even different *magnitudes* of numbers. The two or three largest retrieving engines each often

Table 1.4 Benchmarking Results *cont.*

	Lycos	Northern Light	WebCrawler
Aberystwyth	*	15,701	208
laparoscopy	*	9,014	147
Alvin Toffler	*	**3,719**	46
sidereal messenger	30	**154**	0
Crumpton AND Maryland	97	**256**	3
(trilobite OR trilobites) AND morphology	80	**344**	3
carolingian AND (monastery OR monasteries)	184	584	12

* Engine does not have the functionality to provide a validly comparable answer.

Note that the "winner" for each benchmark is indicated in bold.

For Northern Light, only the Web was searched, not Northern Light's Special Collection.

retrieve more than ten times the number of records retrieved by the smallest retrieving engines.

The primary reasons for the differences in numbers are the size of the database, the quality of the retrieval algorithm, and the depth of indexing of the pages contained in the database. Each of these factors

General Searching Tips

1. Plan your strategy before picking your engine
2. Decide what features would be helpful:
   • Boolean logic?
   • parentheses?
   • proximity?
   • truncation?
   • phrases?
3. Find out which engines provide the features you need (Use Table 1.5—Search Engines Functions Guide, beginning on page 36)
4. Start *specific*, then move *broader* as needed. Get a feel for what's there, then modify your strategy appropriately.
5. Don't hesitate to try different engines and approaches. Try at least two engines unless the first one gives you exactly what you need. If you are looking for a specific fact or a specific page, use one search engine after the other until you find it or decide it's time to give up. If you are looking for "background" and are not sure what you might want, always use at least two search engines.
6. For searching across several engines:
   • Use copy and paste to save and re-use your query. (on PCs: Control-C, Control-V; on Macintoshes: the ⌘-C, ⌘-V keys.
   • When using operators, use upper case characters. For any engine that uses the Boolean operators, upper case will work. Lower case will work with some, but not others. By sticking to upper case, you don't need to worry about which to use.
   • When searching for names, capitalize to make the query more workable across engines.

also contributes to the fact that, for a typical question, each of the larger engines will retrieve records missed by the other large engines.

OVERLAP OF RETRIEVAL BETWEEN ENGINES

One of the most important points that can be made about using Web search engines effectively is the following: **If you are interested in good recall (finding most of the sites that match your needs) you MUST consider searching more than one engine.**

This is not to say that you *always* need to search more than one engine. If you are looking for a specific page, or a specific piece of information and you find it in the first engine you search, wonderful!

However, if you are looking for background material and you are not sure exactly what it is you are after, if you look at the results from one engine and aren't sure you have found the best or most complete answer, you MUST consider searching more than one engine. This can be brought home by an example: Six search engines were searched for the word "melanite." The following were the numbers of distinct records that were retrieved by each:

AltaVista	29
HotBot	28
Infoseek	18
Excite	13
Lycos	1
WebCrawler	1

At first glance there may seem to be one or two "winners." However, an analysis of the individual records showed that there were a total of 52 unique records. Among these 52 records:

- AltaVista found 27 of them, only 52% (coincidentally) of the total group of 52 "relevant" records.
- HotBot found 11 records that were missed by AltaVista
- AltaVista found 17 records missed by HotBot.
- AltaVista and HotBot *together* only found 39 of the 52 records. Together, they still missed 13 of the relevant records.
- To retrieve 90% of the total number of relevant records at

Table 1.5 Search Engines Features Guide
(Blank cell indicates that the feature is not available)
"Window" indicates the option is available in a pull-down window

	AltaVista Simple www.altavista.digital.com	AltaVista **Advanced** www.altavista.digital.com cgi-bin/query?pg=aq
SIZE	140 million	140 million
OR	(Default)	(Default) OR
AND	+word	AND
NOT	-word	AND NOT
PROXIMITY		NEAR
PARENTHESIS		yes
FIELD SEARCHING	yes	yes
PHRASE	" "	" "
TRUNCATION	*	*
NAME		
CASE SENSITIVE	yes	yes
SEARCHES ALL COMMON WORDS	yes	yes
DIRECTORY ATTACHED	yes	yes
GIVES COUNT FOR ANSWER	yes	yes
GIVES TERM COUNT	yes	yes
OUTPUT OPTIONS	Standard	Standard, Count Only
"MORE LIKE THIS"		
SPECIAL FEATURES	Refine Translations	Weighting terms Refine Translations

Table 1.5 Search Engines Features Guide *cont.*
(Blank cell indicates that the feature is not available)
"Window" indicates the option is available in a pull-down window

	Excite Basic www.excite.com	**Excite** Power Search www.excite.com/search/options.html
SIZE	60 million	60 million
OR	(default) OR	(Window)
AND	+word AND	(Window)
NOT	-word AND NOT	(Window)
PROXIMITY		
PARENTHESIS	yes	
FIELD SEARCHING		
PHRASE	" "	(Window)
TRUNCATION	automatic-partial	automatic-partial
NAME		
CASE SENSITIVE		
SEARCHES ALL COMMON WORDS		
DIRECTORY ATTACHED	yes	yes
GIVES COUNT FOR ANSWER	yes	yes
GIVES TERM COUNT		
OUTPUT OPTIONS	summaries titles by website	summaries titles by website
"MORE LIKE THIS"	yes	yes
SPECIAL FEATURES	Automatic thesaurus	Automatic thesaurus

Table 1.5 Search Engines Features Guide *cont.*

(Blank cell indicates that the feature is not available)
"Window" indicates the option is available in a pull-down window

	HotBot www.hotbot.com	Infoseek www.infoseek.com
SIZE	110 million	50 million
OR	Window OR	(Default)
AND	Window AND	+word
NOT	Window NOT	-word
PROXIMITY		
PARENTHESIS	yes	
FIELD SEARCHING	yes	yes
PHRASE	Window " "	" "
TRUNCATION	*	automatic
NAME	Window	yes
CASE SENSITIVE	yes	yes
SEARCHES ALL COMMON WORDS		yes
DIRECTORY ATTACHED	yes	yes
GIVES COUNT FOR ANSWER	yes	yes
GIVES TERM COUNT		
OUTPUT OPTIONS	Full, brief, URL's only 10, 25, 50, 100 results	Hide summaries, Show summaries 10,20,25,50 results
"MORE LIKE THIS"		yes
SPECIAL FEATURES	Search by page depth Can narrow a search	Can NARROW a search

Table 1.5 Search Engines Features Guide *cont.*

(Blank cell indicates that the feature is not available)
"Window" indicates the option is available in a pull-down window

	Lycos (Basic) www.lycos.com	**Lycos Pro Search** w/Java lycospro.lycos.com/lycospro.html
SIZE	35 million	35 million
OR	(Default) Window	OR (Window)
AND	+word	AND (Window)
NOT	-word	NOT (Window)
PROXIMITY		(In "Boolean" Window) ADJ NEAR/n BEFORE FAR OADJ ONEAR OFAR
PARENTHESIS		yes
FIELD SEARCHING		yes
PHRASE	" "	" "
TRUNCATION		
NAME		
CASE SENSITIVE		
SEARCHES ALL COMMON WORDS		
DIRECTORY ATTACHED	yes	
GIVES COUNT FOR ANSWER		
GIVES TERM COUNT		
OUTPUT OPTIONS	Standard	Standard 10, 20, 30, or 40 results
"MORE LIKE THIS"	yes	yes
SPECIAL FEATURES	Can NARROW a search	Can NARROW a search

Table 1.5 Search Engines Features Guide *cont.*
(Blank cell indicates that the feature is not available)
"Window" indicates the option is available in a pull-down window

	Northern Light nlsearch.com	**WebCrawler** webcrawler.com
SIZE	120 million	2 million
OR	OR	(default) OR
AND	+word AND	+word AND
NOT	-word NOT	-word NOT
PROXIMITY		
PARENTHESIS	yes	yes
FIELD SEARCHING	yes	
PHRASE	" "	" "
TRUNCATION	*	
NAME		
CASE SENSITIVE		
SEARCHES ALL COMMON WORDS	yes	
DIRECTORY ATTACHED		yes
GIVES COUNT FOR ANSWER	yes	yes
GIVES TERM COUNT		
OUTPUT OPTIONS	standard	titles summaries
"MORE LIKE THIS"		yes
SPECIAL FEATURES	Special Collection Custom Search Folders, Publication, industry search	Related sites

Table 1.5 Search Engines Features Guide *cont.*
(Blank cell indicates that the feature is not available)
"Window" indicates the option is available in a pull-down window

	Yahoo! www.yahoo.com	
SIZE		
OR	Options checkbox	
AND	+word (default)	
NOT	-word	
PROXIMITY		
PARENTHESIS		
FIELD SEARCHING	yes	
PHRASE	" "	
TRUNCATION	*	
NAME		
CASE SENSITIVE		
SEARCHES ALL COMMON WORDS		
DIRECTORY ATTACHED	**YES**	
GIVES COUNT FOR ANSWER	yes	
GIVES TERM COUNT		
OUTPUT OPTIONS	standard 10, 20, 50, 100	
"MORE LIKE THIS"	By use of classification	
SPECIAL FEATURES	Automatically transfer search to other engines	

least three of the search engines would have to have been searched.

- To retrieve 100% of the total number of relevant records, at least five of the search engines would have to have been searched.

This is just one example, but similar testing using other words produced comparable results.

ABOUT THE PROFILES

Chapters Two through Nine feature profiles of those search engines that are generally considered to be the leading engines in terms of both popularity and searching capabilities. Each profile is designed to allow the searcher to easily know what the engine has to offer and how to take advantage of it. While a major goal was consistency, the unique structure of some of the engines meant that consistency sometimes had to be sacrificed in favor of clarity and completeness.

Most of the facts included in the profiles are from the search engines' online documentation and hundreds of hours spent examining the features and options in detail. Some information came directly from the search engine providers through other means, such as press releases and direct contact. Some of the documentation (the help screens, etc.) from the engines is incomplete and has sometimes even been wrong. An effort is made here to present options and syntax that seem to work (at least most of the time.) When it was not clear that a feature was consistently working, I tended to include it in the expectation that it would be fixed soon. When using search engines be a skeptical optimist: willing to try any of the features, but recognizing that you may not get everything the feature claims to deliver.

Add-Ons

The major add-ons for each engine are listed and/or discussed. No attempt is made to be exhaustive for two reasons: (1) The focus of this book is primarily on the "searching" capabilities of the engines rather than on the sometimes fairly extraneous added features that do not relate directly to the searching of the engine's Web database, and (2) add-ons come and go on a much more frequent basis than the searching features, sometimes on what seems like a daily basis, making information about them rather volatile. The one type of add-on that will be discussed in some detail is the directory. Keep in mind, however, that there are a wide variety of good directories other than those that are attached to search engines. The largest, the most popular, and arguably the best, Yahoo! is covered in Chapter Nine. For a useful listing of other Web directories, take a look at the following category in Yahoo!: "Computers and Internet:Internet:World Wide Web: Searching the Web:Web Directories"

Keeping up with changes in search engines is discussed in Chapter Twelve, and updated information is available on the Web at **www. onstrat.com/engines**.

AltaVista
www.altavista.com <u>or</u> www.av.com

OVERVIEW

AltaVista provides one of the broadest ranges of traditional search functionality of all the major search engines, with Boolean, proximity (NEAR), phrase, date, and field searching, plus truncation. It offers three levels of search sophistication: simple, advanced, and "Refine." With simple and advanced modes, you have the option of searching either the Web or Usenet. AltaVista's home page emphasizes the searching function, with, though, a growing number of add-ons. The differences between simple and

Strengths 👍	Weaknesses 👎
• One of the largest Web databases available • Broad range of traditional search functionality • "Refine" (sophisticated related-terms feature) • Case sensitive • Truncation • Extensive field searching, esp. for URLs • NEAR operator • Translates between English and 5 other languages	• Some problems in the retrieval algorithm (see the warning on page 47) • Gives few cues for using advanced features

advanced search modes can cause some confusion. Most serious searchers will want to stick with the advanced search mode.

AltaVista has indexed about 140 million Web pages.

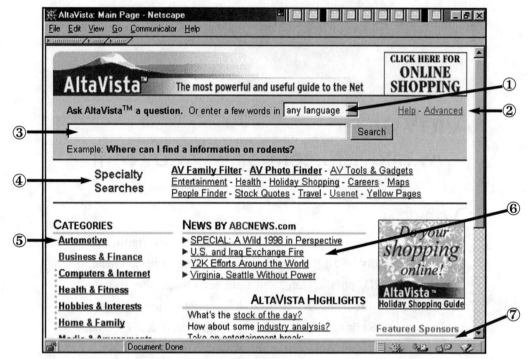

Figure 2.1   The AltaVista home page

① Window for specifying the language in which the page is written
② Link to AltaVista's advanced version
③ Query box for using those options available for simple searching (limited Boolean, etc.)
④ "Specialty Search" links (photos, Usenet, maps, phone directories, etc.)
⑤ Categories (AltaVista's directory, Looksmart)
⑥ Major headlines
⑦ (Below the portion of the screen shown here) "Other Services"; Translations, "Create-a-Card," free email, Asian language search, etc.

WHAT HAPPENS BEHIND THE SCENES

AltaVista indexes all the words in the document (except for "comments") and uses the first few words as a short "abstract."

This abstract takes material from title, URL, metatags (description and keywords up to 1,024 characters), headers (for Usenet articles), the text of the page, links, image names, ALT text for images, etc. Punctuation is not indexed. According to the AltaVista documentation, "In the absence of any other information, AltaVista will index all words in a document (except for comments), and will use the first few words of the document as a short abstract." Daily, AltaVista visits sites submitted by users (ca. 20,000/day) and it "continuously crawls and indexes the 2,000 most active sites on the Web as well as selected public service and government sites."

During indexing, AltaVista uses a technology that converts documents into Unicode, a standard encoding that allows the system to deal with most of the world's languages and character sets. Most significantly, this allows pages in non-Roman alphabets to be effectively indexed and retrieved.

AltaVista first searches to find "matches," then "ranks" them for output.

WARNING! When performing searches involving heavily used terms, it has been shown that AltaVista does not necessarily retrieve all matching records. There have also been times when results numbers for the same search, done within minutes, may differ significantly.

Source: Hock, "Do Search Engines Deliver What they Promise," Paper presented at Online World, New York, Sept. 15, 1997

If just a string of terms is entered, AltaVista will "OR" all of the terms and deliver them in the order determined by the ranking algorithm.

Documents are assigned a score for ranking purposes based on:

- How many of your search terms are present in the document.
- Proximity of the query words or phrases to each other
- Where in the page the search terms occur

Stop words: AltaVista indexes all words. In effect, however, because of the retrieval algorithm, most common words are ignored when AltaVista's default (non-Boolean) mode is used.

AltaVista's Simple Search

AltaVista's "Simple Search" employs many of the features of its "Advanced Search." The main differences are:

- The lesser degree to which Boolean logic can be used in simple search
- One less output option ("count only") in simple search
- In simple search there is no date range search box

What AltaVista's Simple Search Does with Queries

For Simple Search queries, AltaVista will "OR" the words together. Output is ordered by relevance. If however, you enter two or more terms that are found in AltaVista's "phrase dictionary," the words will be searched automatically as a phrase.

Boolean Logic in AltaVista's Simple Search

+word   Put a plus sign immediately in front of the term to insist that a word be present (+word acts as an AND).

-word   Put a minus sign immediately in front of the term to exclude records with that word (-word acts as a NOT).

Example: +elephants -circus

Truncation in AltaVista's Simple Search

*   Use an asterisk to truncate a search phrase.

     Example: Mexic*

At least three preceding letters are required. The asterisk will match from 0–5 additional lower case letters—not capital letters or digits (a search for engin* will not retrieve "engineering"). The asterisk can be used internally (e.g., lab*r will retrieve both labor and labour). If too many matches are found, AltaVista will ignore the word (and tell you it did so).

Phrase Searching in AltaVista's Simple Search

" "   Use double quotation marks to search on a phrase.

     Example: "Great Britain"

Any punctuation has the same effect as the use of the quotation marks—e.g., the following three are equivalent:

     "frontal lobotomy"
     frontal-lobotomy
     frontal;lobotomy

The above three variations are a case of a feature being "there" with no apparent advantage actually accruing from its presence. Just stick with using quotation marks as in the other search engines.

AltaVista now automatically recognizes millions of commonly used phrases. When two or more words are entered that match a phrase in this list, the string is automatically searched as a phrase. To be safe, if you want to search a phrase, go ahead and use the quotation marks anyway in case your phrase isn't on AltaVista's phrase list.

Name Searching and Case Sensitivity in AltaVista's Simple Search

To search for proper names, take advantage of the fact that AltaVista can distinguish cases. Search for Scott Brand, instead of scott brand, if you want the person by that name. (Realistically, for how many people is this an issue?)

Searching in all lower case will get both upper and lower case. For example, "aids" will retrieve aids, AIDS, Aids, aiDs, etc.

If you use capital letters in a search it will force an exact case match for the entire word. For example, "eTRUST" will retrieve "eTRUST" but not "eTrust."

As well as being case-sensitive, AltaVista is also sensitive to accent marks and other diacritical marks, allowing you to distinguish if necessary. (If you want to search on diacritics, the problem will be finding them on your keyboard or finding the keyboard codes that represent them. A work-around is to find the appropriate character in a document, then "copy and paste" it into the query).

Field Searching in AltaVista's Simple Search

The field searching options for simple and advanced search modes are identical. See the discussion of this under "AltaVista Advanced Search. " (Note that anyone needing the level of sophistication provided by AltaVista's field search capabilities should be using the advanced search version anyway.)

ALTAVISTA'S ADVANCED SEARCH

AltaVista's "Advanced Search" provides virtually all of the options of the simple search mode, plus considerably greater functionality in terms of full Boolean logic and date searching.

Boolean Logic in AltaVista's Advanced Search

In Advanced Search mode, when terms are entered in the main query box with no other specified criteria, AltaVista will "OR" the terms or, if the words are found in AltaVista's phrase dictionary, it will search the words as a phrase. Be aware, though, that because of the way the retrieval algorithm works, records that do indeed match may be missed. Some records in the database that should be retrieved are not retrieved.

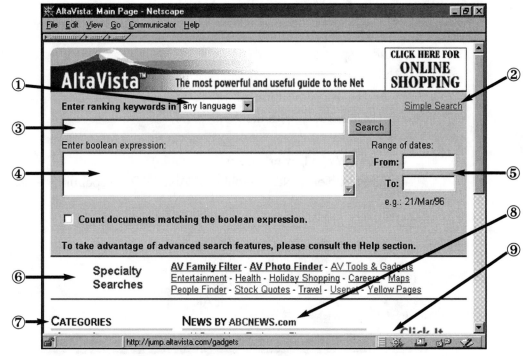

Figure 2.2   AltaVista's Advanced Search screen

① Window for specifying the language in which the page is written

② Link to AltaVista's Simple version

③ Query box for entering keywords

④ Box for entering Boolean queries

⑤ Boxes for entering a date range

⑥ "Specialty Search" links (photos, Usenet, maps, phone directories, etc.)

⑦ AltaVista's Categories (LookSmart directory)

⑧ Major headlines

⑨ (Below the area shown on this screen):

    Options for:

    Alta Vista's Discovery software download

    Free email

    Translation service

    Create-a-card

    Photo albums

    Asian language search

The following operators can be used:

AND

OR

NEAR

AND NOT—Be sure to use AND NOT, instead of NOT, and don't start the query with the AND NOT.

( )

(*Author's Note:* Lower case is acceptable)

Example: diet* AND "weight loss" AND NOT grapefruit*

Alternatively, the following could be used:

&	for	AND
|	for	OR
!	for	NOT
~	for	NEAR

Get in the habit of using upper case for operators, since this works in all search engines that allow Boolean operators. This way, you won't have to worry about which engines do or do not require capitalization.

Because the words AND, OR, AND NOT, and the above symbols are interpreted as operators, if you want to use them as search terms, place them in quotes.

As you will notice from the Advanced Search screen, Boolean statements must be placed in the "Boolean expression" query box. If you place them in the first box, it won't work. Also, be aware that when you use a Boolean expression in AltaVista (as with other search engines), results will no longer be ranked by relevance. AltaVista's documentation indicates that you can put an expression in the Boolean expression box and in the same search also put terms you wish to use for ranking in the main box. However, contrary to the documentation, what actually seems to happen is that the terms you enter in the main query box get "ANDed" with your Boolean statement. Until this gets fixed, if you use Boolean, don't put anything in the main query box.

Truncation in AltaVista's Advanced Search

*   Use an asterisk to truncate a search term (requires at least three preceding letters).

This will match from 0–5 additional lower case letters—not capital letters or digits (a search for engin* will not retrieve "engineering"). The asterisk can be used internally (for instance, lab*r will retrieve both labor and labour). If too many matches are found, AltaVista will ignore the word (and tell you it did so).

Phrases and Proximity Searching in AltaVista's Advanced Search

Use double quotation marks to search on a phrase.

Example: "common law"

As mentioned before, AltaVista now automatically matches word strings against its dictionary of commonly used phrases. If a match is found, the string is automatically searched as a phrase. The safe thing to do for phrases to go ahead and use the quotation marks anyway in case your phrase isn't on AltaVista's phrase list.

Any punctuation has the same effect as quotation marks—e.g., the following three are equivalent:

       "frontal lobotomy"
       frontal-lobotomy
       frontal;lobotomy

NEAR - specifies that the two terms must occur within ten words of each other.

Example: chips NEAR prices

Name Searching and Case Sensitivity in AltaVista's Advanced Search

To search names, take advantage of the fact that AltaVista can distinguish cases (search for Scott Brand, instead of scott brand, if you want the person by that name).

Searching in all lower cases will get both upper and lower case. For example, "aids" will retrieve aids, AIDS, Aids, aiDs, etc. If you use capital letters in a search it will force an exact case match for the entire word. For example, "eTRUST" will retrieve "eTRUST" but not "eTrust." As well as being case-sensitive, AltaVista is also sensitive to accent marks and other diacritical marks, allowing you to distinguish if necessary.

Field Searching in AltaVista's Advanced Search

AltaVista currently has the longest list of specifically searchable fields (though the usefulness of some is minimal except perhaps to programmers). The following techniques yield results in both simple and advanced search modes. In Advanced mode, use the following in the Boolean expression box, not in the main query box.

title:"Boston Globe"	Searches for words or phrases in a page title.
anchor:"click here"	Searches words within links (anchors).
text:colchester	Finds pages that contain the specified word "in any part of the visible text of a page" (i.e., the word is not in a link, image, or the URL).
applet:NervousText	Searches for specific applets.

object:Marquee	Searches for (programming) "objects."
link:thomas.gov	Finds pages that link to the specified page (for a discussion of the ways in which this type of feature can be used, see the chapter on HotBot)
image:beetle.jpg	Searches the word in the file name of an image (extension optional).
url:sec.gov	Searches any contiguous portions of a URL.
host:digital.com	Searches for pages within the specified host.
domain:fr	Searches for the specific domain (country domains such as fr for France and institutional domains such as .com, .edu, etc.)

Field Searching in Usenet News Articles in AltaVista's Advanced Search

from:jsmith@onstrat.com

subject:"for sale" (you can combine this with a word or phrase. For example: subject:"for sale" AND "beanie babies")

newsgroups:rec.humor

summary:invest*

keywords:NASA

For both the Web and Usenet searching, truncation can be used with these prefixes.

Example: image:beetle*

Date Searching in AltaVista's Advanced Search

In Advanced Search mode, AltaVista allows you to specify a date range, using the date text box. The date should be entered in the following format:

22/Apr/97

Language Option in AltaVista's Advanced Search

Using the pull-down window provided in both simple and advanced mode, you can specify that you only want pages written in one of twenty-five languages. The default is "all languages."

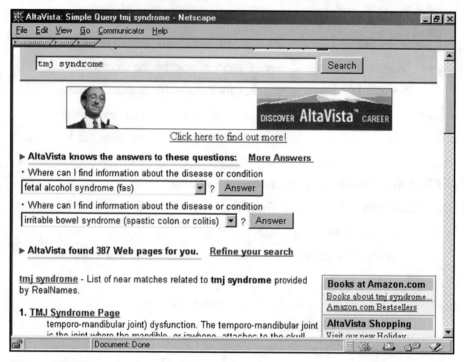

Figure 2.3   Example of an AltaVista results page

OUTPUT

Output Report Statement— AltaVista's Simple and Advanced Search

AltaVista reports results as:

> AltaVista found about 268 Web pages for you.

In the Simple mode (but not in the Advanced mode), the number of records displayed is limited to 200.

Output Formats—
AltaVista's Simple and Advanced Search

AltaVista offers only one format option in Simple mode. In Advanced mode it also offers the option of receiving only a count of records.

Sample Record:

1. CEPR Perspectives
   THE CENTER FOR ECONOMIC POLICY RESEARCH Stanford University. CEPR
   PERSPECTIVES. The following articles are highlights of recent issues of CEPR's...
   URL: www-cepr.stanford.edu/CEPR_Publications/Perspectives.htm
   Last modified 10-Jul-98 - page size 80K - in English [Translate]

As a Count Only (available in Advanced Search):

AltaVista found about 38819 Web pages for you.

OTHER OPTIONS ON RESULTS PAGES

On results pages, for some searches, AltaVista now presents some interesting options in addition to the actual Web results. In its Simple version, AltaVista presents the option of searching the RealName database of official company and product home pages. If you are indeed looking for a company or product, and if the company has paid to subscribe to RealName, you are in luck. This is a convenient shortcut to getting to a company's home page and to quickly getting product information.

For some searches, AltaVista will present a list of searches (phrases) similiar to your own search that you may want to consider searching. These will appear immediately under the query box on your results page. For example, a search on Bauhaus suggested such phrases as Bauhaus furniture, Bauhaus Resurrection, and Bauhaus Dessau. These suggestions can be particularly useful for ideas for narrowing a search.

For many searches in AltaVista's simple mode, especially those involving commonly searched terms, geographic names, etc., AltaVista enlists the Ask Jeeves search service. On results pages, you may see a question presented (involving your term) to which AltaVista "knows the answer." These questions and answers come from the "answers" database created and maintained by Ask Jeeves (also available directly at **aj.com**).

If your search term appeared in an entry in the LookSmart directory listings, AltaVista may also suggest the relevant directory category. Clicking on the link provided there may take you to some other sites you may wish to consider.

SPECIAL OPTIONS

Translate

AltaVista, in cooperation with SYSTRAN Translation Software, now offers an immediate machine translation of the Web page by clicking on the "**Translate**" link at the end of a record. It will translate either way between English and French, German, Italian, Portuguese, or Spanish. This feature is available in both the simple and advanced versions of AltaVista. In the record below for a page originally in French, by clicking on the "**Translate**" link at the end of the record, the translation screen will appear:

2. Elections - Le Progres - CANTON DE ROCHEFORT-SUR-NENON
CANTON DE ROCHEFORT-SUR-NENON. 3. 2. BARBIER. VOYNET. COMMUNES. Inscrits. Votants. Exprimes. (UDF) (Verts PS) Amange. 217. 175. 160. 66. 94. Archelange ...
URL: www.leprogres.fr/elections/39LG2034.htm
Last modified 9-Aug-98 - page size 3K - in French [Translate]

Additionally, by clicking on the "**Translate**" tab on the home page, you can enter any URL, or for that matter any text, and have it translated.

Set Your Preferences

The Set Your Preferences link found at the bottom of pages allows you to change to the Advanced version of AltaVista as your default, a choice of language encoding for query entry, choice of language output (as in the "languages" box on the query screen), choice of the graph version as the default for Refine results, and text-only output for those who don't use a graphical browser.

ADD-ONS

In both the simple and advanced versions, AltaVista presents a number of add-ons. AltaVista has the habit of significantly redesigning its pages every few months, so you may have to look around a bit to find these.

- The translation program—this is integrated into the results output and is also available independently of search results. See the preceding discussion of the translation feature for details.
- LookSmart, a directory ("Categories")—see the section on the directory at the end of this chapter.
- "People Finder"—uses Switchboard's people directory for addresses, phone numbers, etc.
- "Yellow Pages"—uses Switchboard's business directory to find addresses, phone numbers, etc.
- Health—a channel for health-related links and information.
- Entertainment—a channel for entertainment-related information.
- Travel—a travel channel, from TheTrip.com, for fares, flights, hotel reservations, maps, etc.
- Stock Quotes—a finance channel providing a variety of free information such as stock quotes, news, company overviews, portfolio tracking, interactive performance charts, etc., plus research reports on a pay-per-view basis.
- AV Photo Finder—an easy-to-use database of over 10 million images from the Corbis collection, the Web, and other sources.
- AV Family Filter—allows filtering of objectionable material.
- AV Tools & Gadgets—a useful collection of links for a variety of calculators, directories, shipping and postal information, travel, etc.
- Maps—maps and driving directions, powered by Vicinity Corporation.
- Usenet—search items posted to newsgroups in the last two weeks using the AltaVista interface (see earlier section on Field searching).

- Free Email—free email services.
- News—news headlines from ABCNEWS.com
- AltaVista Discovery—provides a downloadable "local" version of the AltaVista program for searching both the Web and local files.
- Careers—a collection of career-related links, including advice, job postings, etc.
- RealName: This feature (which you will find a link for on results pages) allows you to search a database of company names, products, trademarks, etc. to quickly locate the home page for a company.
- Create A Card: A search of 500,000 images from the Corbis collection, which allows not only a search of images, but also the creation of greeting cards using those images. Users should keep in mind that these images are copyrighted, as are most other images found on the Web.

AltaVista Refine

"Refine" is AltaVista's sophisticated text analysis technique, which can be used in conjunction with either Simple or Advanced Search. To use the Refine option, click on the "Refine your search" link that appears on results pages. The results represent the co-occurrence of terms. It is to some degree like a "thesaurus on the fly," showing a collection of related terms. By clicking on the related words identified by Refine, those words can be included in the query either as an AND or a NOT.

Results of Refine can be viewed either in list or graph form. The latter is available only if you have a Java-enabled browser. The list version is the default, but you can see the graph version either by clicking on "Graph" when in the List mode or by setting that choice in your preferences.

Refine can be used to:

- Identify related terms
- Easily add additional concepts

- Eliminate terms frequently encountered but not relevant to your search
- Get a "picture" of the subject area

Refine Results—List Version

In the screen that appears in Figure 2.4, the term "cryogenic" had been entered on AltaVista's home page and then the **Refine** button clicked. On the page that was returned, the term "superconducting" was clicked to show how the user has the option of either including (**AND**ing) the term or excluding (**NOT**ing) the term. When you do so for one or more of the terms and click "Search," a revised search is set in motion. If you click the **Refine** button, a new version of the table (graph) will be generated.

If you see a term that would be useful as a synonym (alternate term) for one of the concepts in your search statement, click the

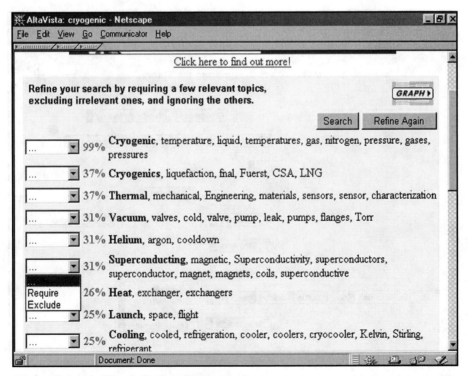

Figure 2.4   AltaVista's Refine (list version)

Search button (on the Refine results page) then add the word manually to your query in the query box.

The percentages shown represent AltaVista's calculation of probable relevance.

With Refine, the terms ("topics") are generated based on which terms frequently "co-occur" with the terms for which you searched. Topics are listed by order of "relevance." Words within topics are listed by frequency of occurrence.

AltaVista, and an elementary understanding of statistics, suggest that a larger initial retrieval set will result in a better topic map.

Note that for the cryogenic example in Figure 2.4, when the plural ("cryogenics") was used a very different map resulted.

Refine Results—Graph Version

The "Graph" version of Refine presents a much more graphic view of the term relationships.

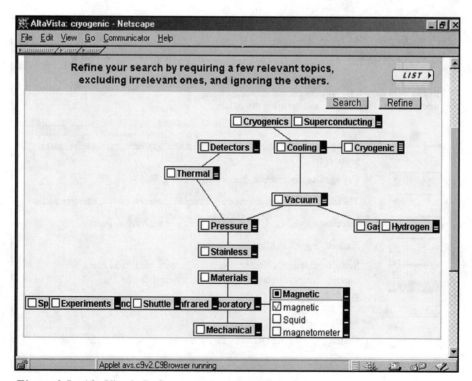

Figure 2.5 AltaVista's Refine (graph version)

In the screen shown in Figure 2.5, "Magnetic" was clicked. Clicking once on any term will AND it, clicking twice will NOT it.

> **Consider using Refine as a way of preparing even for non-Web searches. Also, try it with a company name.**

ALTAVISTA'S DIRECTORY—LOOKSMART

Overview of LookSmart

AltaVista offers a classified directory of over 600,000 pages through a partnership with LookSmart (which is also available directly at http://looksmart.com). The directory is located under "Categories" on both the Simple and Advanced search pages. (HotBot also has partnered with LookSmart and is using the same directory. For the reader's convenience, and because of differences in the implementation, a discussion of LookSmart also appears in the HotBot chapter.)

Searchability of LookSmart

LookSmart can be searched, but, with a few exceptions, the searches are "all-or-nothing," i.e., it allows a search of the entire directory but does not allow searching within a specified category. When you are at LookSmart's top level page, or at the bottom level of any category, a search box is provided. When a search is entered there, LookSmart returns first the matching sites from the LookSmart collection, then matching sites from "the entire Web."

There are a few (very few) exceptions to the statement that subcategories are not searchable. Occasionally you may encounter a magnifying glass icon at a subcategory level, such as the "Destinations" subcategory within "Travel and Vacations." By clicking on one of these subcategories you will be taken to a specialized search.

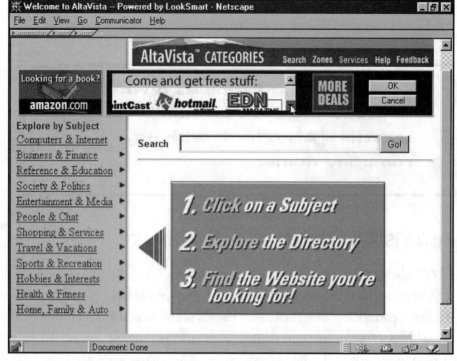

Figure 2.6   Top level of AltaVista's directory categories

Structure of the LookSmart Directory

LookSmart's thirteen main categories, shown in Figure 2.6, contain over 24,000 subcategories and 600,000 pages. For most of the categories, there are three or four additional levels of hierarchy.

In Figure 2.7, the "Society & Politics" category was selected, then within that, the "Int'l Affairs" category. To the right of "Development & Relief" is a page symbol that indicates that there are no more categories. Clicking on "Development & Relief" will lead to a listing of actual Web sites, rather than another subcategory. The arrow to the right of "Organizations" indicates that there are further subcategories.

LookSmart's top levels are:

- Automotive
- Business & Finance

Figure 2.7 AltaVista/LookSmart screen shot: Society & Politics

- Computers & Internet
- Health & Fitness
- Hobbies & Interests
- Home & Family
- Media & Amusements
- People & Chat
- Reference & Education
- Shopping & Services
- Society & Politics
- Sports & Recreation
- Travel & Vacations

Examples of levels and sublevels are:

Business & Finance
    Int'l Business
        Countries and Regions

> Asia
>
> Regional Information
>
> Reference & Education
>
> K-12 Education
>
> Schools on the Net
>
> Elementary Schools
>
> States A-D

A query box appears on the *top level* LookSmart page and also on pages at the *bottom of a hierarchy* (see Figure 2.8). Keep in mind that a search entered here is searching the entire LookSmart database, not just the current subcategory.

Beneath the search box is a summary line indicating where you are in the classification hierarchy. You can return to a level of your choice by clicking on the appropriate place in this summary line. "World" refers to LookSmart's top level.

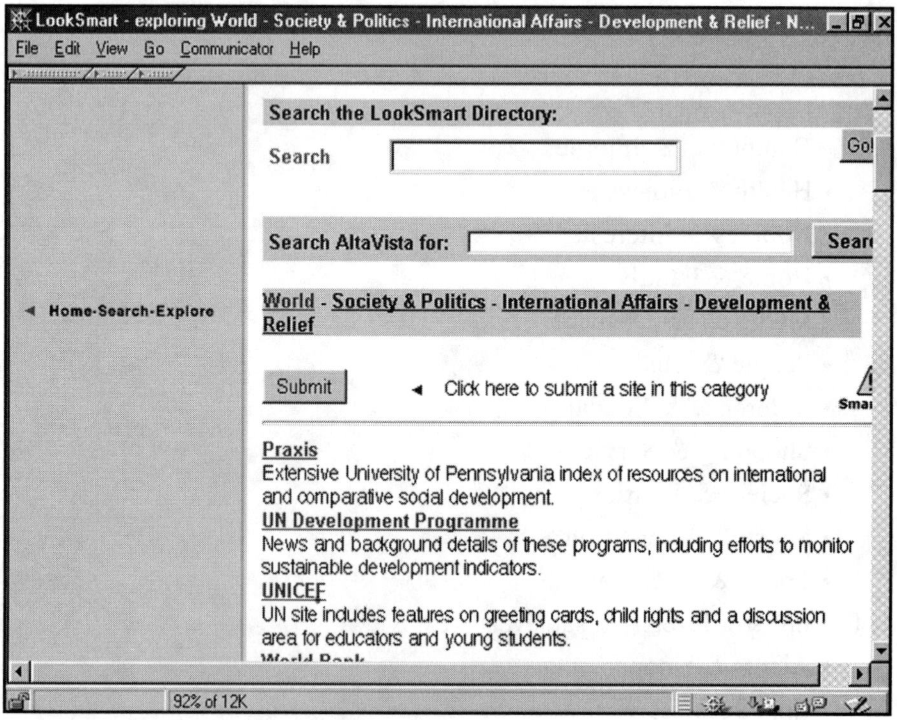

Figure 2.8   Fourth-level LookSmart directory listings

Special Features in LookSmart

Special Symbols Used:

- A blue arrowhead to the right of a category name indicates the level that you expanded, or for the level you're now on, the fact that a subcategory has one or more additional levels available.
- Clicking on a subcategory that shows a "page" icon will lead to an "site list" (i.e., a listing of actual sites, rather than another subcategory listing).
- A white exclamation mark in a red box indicates a new category, or a "site list" that contains new listings, i.e., pages recently added to the directory.
- A magnifying glass indicates a page that has its own specialized searchable index.

Pages/sites can be submitted to LookSmart by clicking the "Click here to submit a site in this category" link on site listing pages.

SUMMARY OF ALTAVISTA

AltaVista is one of the two largest and most powerful Web search engines. It has a very broad range of functionality and features. The translation and Refine features are unique, powerful, and useful. AltaVista's main weaknesses are that some features do not do what they are supposed to do and for some features (such as field searching), neither the availability of the feature nor instructions on how to use it are shown on the home page. This and other design choices seem to be made by programmers or marketers who assume that users don't care about sophisticated searching. Nevertheless, AltaVista is a service that serious searchers should use extensively, and they should explore the variety of powerful tools AltaVista provides.

For any search where it is important that relevant items not be missed, AltaVista, along with HotBot, Northern Light, and maybe one or two others, should always be searched.

Excite
www.excite.com

OVERVIEW

As a search engine, Excite is in the mid-range functionally. It has full Boolean capabilities and phrase searching, but no field searching or truncation options. It is unique among the major engines in terms of its capability to retrieve information based on its automated thesaurus. This thesaurus is generated by analysis of the content of all indexed Web pages, which Excite then uses to identify related terminology. Excite's "**More Like This**" link in (some) retrieved records allows users to expand their search based on similarity to the selected record. The "Power Search" version allows more choice in *what* is searched (Web, News, etc.), but allows less flexibility for Boolean.

Strengths 👍	Weaknesses 👎
• Automated thesaurus • Option of "selected" sites • "More like this" feature • Personalizable home page • Strong current awareness capability	• No user-controlled truncation • No field searching • "Power-Search" mode actually the less-powerful mode • Only a medium-sized database

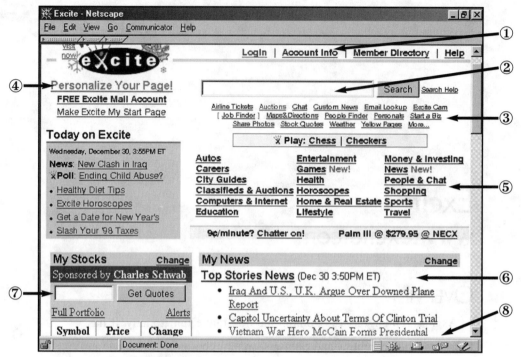

Figure 3.1   Excite's home page

① **Login** and account information for personalized version

② **Query Box**—Words, Boolean expressions, etc., can be entered.

③ **Add-ons**—Yellow Pages, People Finder, Maps and Directions, Email Lookup, Job Finder, Weather, etc.

④ **Personalizing Option**—for personalized selection of content, layout, and colors of the Excite home page

⑤ **"Channels"**—Excite's directory

⑥ **Headlines**—Top Stories, Business, Technology, Sports, etc.

⑦ **Stocks**—Quotes, portfolio, etc.

⑧ (At the bottom of the page, not shown in figure)

> **NewsTracker Topics**
> **Chat**
> **Horoscope**
> **Sports**
> **Weather**
> **Links to Global Excite**
> **Link to Power Search mode**
> **Etc.**

Beyond the searching function, Excite stands out from the pack with the emphasis the home page places on news and personalization. In 1998, Excite shifted from trying to be an America Online look-alike to a look and feel of its own, providing a home page that any user can tailor to his or her own needs, especially in terms of headline news. Excite still has "channels," but, whereas they previously received top billing, they are now relegated to a minor role and occupy only a small section of the Excite home page.

Excite has indexed about 60 million Web pages.

Additional features, including sports scores and TV listings, can also be selected by the user to appear on the personalized home page.

With Excite You Can Search:

The Web, in either Excite's home page version or Power Search. Or, using Power Search:

- Selected Web Sites
- Current News
- Excite Germany, Excite France, Excite UK, Excite Sweden

When the Power Search link (hidden near the bottom of Excite's home page) is clicked, you see the screen represented in Figure 3.2 (see page 72).

WHAT HAPPENS BEHIND THE SCENES

Excite has created (and continually modifies) an automatic thesaurus, based on word and concept relationships (e.g., co-occurrence). Its proprietary term for this process is "ICE" (Intelligent Concept Extraction). When you do a search, Excite uses ICE to identify theoretically related sites.

While it does index text found in tables, Excite does not index some metatags. Depending on how solid their retrieval algorithm is, this could be a major drawback.

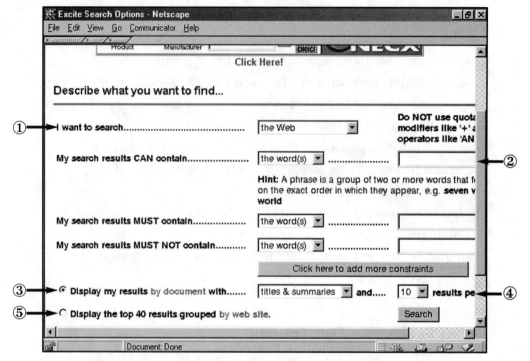

Figure 3.2   Excite's Power Search screen

Excite's Power Search provides the same options as the home page version, plus:

① The ability to choose to search:

   • **The Web**

   • **Selected Web Sites**—those included in Excite's channels directory, which contains 140,000 selected listings. 60,000 of these are linked to reviews written by Excite editors

   • **Current News**—from Reuters and over 300 Web-based publications

   • **Excite Germany, Excite France, Excite UK, Excite Sweden**—The country-specific versions of Excite

② The ability to OR, AND and NOT words or phrases by using pull-down window choices, instead of the operators themselves. Note that this approach (windows) does not allow searching of an expression equivalent to: (Mexico OR Mexican) AND (chemical OR petroleum)

③ The option of displaying:

   • Titles only

   • Titles and summaries

④ The option of displaying 10, 20, 30, 40 or 50 records per page

⑤ The ability to display the top 40 results by Web site

Excite does not index frames or crawl links found in frames. This is a major drawback. In Excite, sites with frames may be indexed simply by title and/or URL. 👎

If a string of terms is entered with no qualifiers (such as Boolean operators), Excite will "OR" all of the words. Retrieved records are sorted by relevance.

SEARCH FEATURES

Boolean logic

In conjunction with the default "concept" search, you can use the following options, but only with the home page version, not in Power Search mode:

+word Put a plus sign immediately in front of the term to insist that a word be present

-word Put a minus sign immediately in front of the term to exclude records with that word.

> *Example*: +java -coffee

Boolean (Full)

On the Excite Home Page (again, not in Power Search) you can use the following Boolean operators listed. When you do, concept-based retrieval is turned off. When using these operators, Excite requires capitalization.

> AND
> OR
> AND NOT
> ( )
>> *Example*:
>> (Web OR Internet) AND searching AND NOT Lycos

Truncation

Truncation is not available *per se*, but the effect is achieved (somewhat) in the concept-based searching done automatically by the Excite program. Remember that when you use the Boolean AND, OR, or NOT, the concept-based retrieval is turned off. Therefore when those connectors are used, the safe thing to do is to specifically enter the variant endings.

Phrases

" "   Use double quotation marks (use of this does not turn off concept-based retrieval)

         Example: "Bill Gates"

Name Searching

A specific "name searching" feature is not available. Use phrase searching (" ") to accomplish a name search.

Field Searching

Excite provides no field searching capabilities.

OUTPUT

Format Options

Choice of output formats can be made in Simple mode only after a results page has been displayed. In Power Mode, formats can be selected from a pull-down window. In either mode, the format options are: Show Summaries, Show Titles Only, and List by Web Site. The "List by Web site" option is unique to Excite and is useful when encountering a large number of pages from the same site. Arranging retrieved pages by site makes it easier for a searcher to determine the source of the information, and thus its potential relevance. The percentage shown in each record is the relevance "score" assigned by Excite's retrieval program.

Show Summaries

72% <u>Chemical Processing, July 1996</u> - As the largest manufacturing sector in terms of added value, the U.S. chemical industry produces nearly 2% of the total GNP and nearly 9% of manufacturing's value-added GNP. In this era of an ever-increasing

national trade deficit, the U.S. chemical industry provides more than 10 cents of every dollar of exports, and during the 10-year period ending in 1994 amassed a cumulative trade surplus.
http:///www.chemicalprocessing.com/protected/cp796/edpage1.sh...
Search for more documents like this one

Show Titles Only
73% Chemical Engineering Organization Info Auburn University Alabama [More Like This]

List by Web Site
www.cmahq.com
99% CMA: Membership Affiliates [More Like This]
90% CMA: About CMA [More Like This]

www.neis.com
93% The Chemical Industry Home Page [More Like This]

logistx.dartgc.com
90% NewsGram Oct 96: Council of chemical Logistics Providers [More Like This]

"More Like This"

You will notice that after each record is a "search for more documents like this one" link. When you click on this link, Excite's program analyzes the record and identifies other records that have similar or related terminology (using the ICE algorithm described earlier.)

Search Wizard

In "Simple" mode, when results are shown, Excite lists up to ten additional terms for the user to consider. Excite refers to this as the Search Wizard. The related terms identified when "downsizing AND productivity" was searched are shown in Figure 3.3 (see page 76). Many times the related terms identified by Excite will be right on target. At other times they are somewhat puzzling. The Search Wizard does, however, usually produce at least some terms that you may wish to consider for refining or expanding your search.

News and Other Related Records

Starting first with company and sports searches, Excite has begun augmenting Web output with additional records from news sources, listings from Excite's directory, sports scores, stock prices, etc. This has been implemented primarily as an enhancement for very simple, often single-term, searches. Excite plans to continue adding to the categories of searches to which this will be applied.

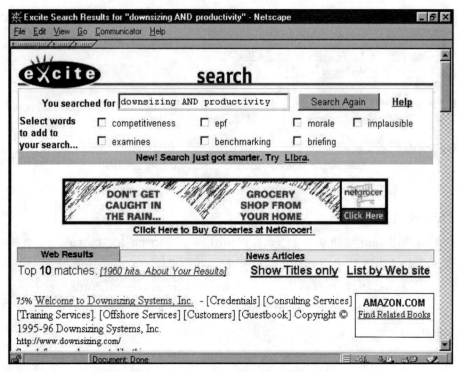

Figure 3.3 ***An Excite results page showing related terms identified when searching on "downsizing AND productivity"***

ADD-ONS

Personalization Options

Excite's new philosophy is centered around providing an information service that allows the user to extensively personalize what is seen on the Excite home page. Searching is but one aspect that the user can choose. Though this book aims to concentrate primarily on the searching aspects of the major search engine services, in order to adequately describe what Excite is all about it is necessary to go into somewhat more detail than usual about this engine's range of offerings, particularly the personalizable features. Also, some of Excite's added features have a searching function of their own, most notably the NewsTracker service, which provides an easy-to-use, yet rather full-featured news alerting (current-awareness) service.

I suppose I should confess something here. While Excite is not usually my first choice for a Web search, I have selected its home page as the default page for my browser. By going directly to my personalized Excite page when I log on, I can see news headlines on topics of interest to me, check the shape of my meager stock portfolio, and—most importantly—with a single click I can get the latest news relevant to any one of several personally tailored current awareness searches (currently included, as you might suspect, is one on "search engines").

Most of the sections of the Excite home page are personalizable in terms of specific content and location on the page. A brief description of the more significant of these personalizable sections follows.

Headline News

In the "Headline News" section, by clicking on the "Change" button you can elect to have headlines displayed from the following broad topics, or from numerous subcategories within those topics. You can also specify the order in which they are listed.

•Top Stories	•Business	•Sports News
•Technology	•Political	•International
•Oddly Enough	•Industries	•News by State
• Entertainment		

Stocks

Excite's "Stocks" section allows you to track market indices, or to create your own detailed portfolio of holdings and then view them in any one of several formats. (Excite uses Charles Schwab for this service.)

Reminders

You can choose to be reminded of holidays and other events, or add your own events and specify how far before the event you wish to be reminded. A small notepad can also be included.

Weather

Utilizing your Zip Code, Excite will provide your local weather report. You can also get a report on tides, sunrise and sunset, and the moon.

Favorite Links

"Favorite Links" is a bookmarks-like feature.

Sports Scores

Excite offers both a chart of current sports action and a sports scores ticker.

NewsTracker

"NewsTracker" is an optional category in the news section that deserves special attention because of its relevance to searching. NewsTracker is a free "clipping service" that accesses over 300 sources, including major newswires, magazines, and newspapers. With NewsTracker it is easy to set up to twenty current awareness searches to enable you to easily keep up with news events relating to topics of interest. In setting up searches, full Boolean is not available, but **+word** can be used as an AND, and **-word** as a NOT. NewsTracker is a service most serious searchers will want to explore.

Other optional sections of the personalized page include horoscopes, TV listings, movies, and cartoons.

Most sections of Excite's home page are personalizable in various ways. In addition, users can determine the order in which selected options appear on the screen and the color schemes used.

Other Add-Ons

In various locations on the page, you will find numerous and frequently changing add-ons. Among others, these include:

- Yellow Pages—Uses Zip2 business phone directory
- People Finder—Uses the AT&T White Pages directory of U.S. phone numbers and addresses, with a few links to other directories
- Maps & Directions—For driving directions, mapping an address, or browsing road maps
- Classifieds—Search or place free classified ads
- Email Lookup—Uses the WhoWhere? email directory
- More—A modest-sized, but well-organized collection of links to various directories and reference tools.
- PAL Instant Paging—"Free Instant Paging," for finding friends who are currently online
- Newsgroups—Links to Deja News, which provides access to more than 50,000 newsgroups
- Global Excite—Country specific versions for Australia, France, Germany, Japan, Netherlands, Sweden and the UK (plus a Chinese language version). Certainly if you are in these countries, you may want to make use of these versions, but even if you are not, but are doing research on non-U.S. companies, consider these sites. They contain information you may not find on the generic Excite.

In addition, there are links for adding an Excite button to your browser toolbar, bookmarking Excite, adding your URL, etc.

Regarding add-ons in general, for Excite and other services the alliances between search engines and the companies that provide the add-ons are constantly shifting. Be prepared to see frequent changes both in the types of add-ons and in the companies providing them.

EXCITE'S DIRECTORY

Overview of Excite's Directory (Channels)

Excite's directory is tucked away on the pages of the individual channels, which themselves are now given much less prominence than in the earlier version of Excite. To get to the directory, you first have to look carefully for the channel listings on the Excite home page, then once in a channel you have to look carefully to see the list of further categories. The categories are most often at the left of a channel page with the channel's special features and services on the right. Each channel contains a selection of services ranging from sports scores to interest rates, from message boards to chat rooms. Figure 3.4 (see page 82) provides an example, showing the page from the **Education** channel. This page is at the **Universities and Colleges** sublevel. Additional subcategories are shown on the left under "**Directory.**" (The listings of the next level categories are not always so clearly labeled. For example, in the **Computers and Internet** channel, the next level down is labeled "**Departments.**")

The directory, formerly referred to as the "**Web Guide,**" contains 140,000 sites, 25,000 of which have been reviewed by Excite editors.

The content of the Excite channels is more consumer than research-oriented. The **Money & Investing** and **Careers & Education** channels contain significant substance for the serious searcher, but most of the other channels seem targeted toward the serious couch potato. There is little evidence of sites related to arts and humanities, science, engineering, etc.

Searchability of Excite's Directory

Interestingly, the only readily apparent way to search the contents of Excite's directory is not to go to the directory itself, but to go to **Power Search.** There, one can choose **Selected Web Sites** in the "**I want to search...**" box, and the entire directory is searched. Except for "**News,**" the channels are not individually searchable.

Many do, though, have associated specialized searching capabilities, such as for stock quotes in the Business & Investing channel.

In some cases, at the bottom of a directory page a search box may appear that will allow you to search the Excite Web database. However, this option is not available for a large number of directory pages.

Structure of the Directory

Excite's directory is organized into eighteen top level channels:

- Autos
- Careers
- City Guides
- Classifieds/Auctions
- Computers/Internet
- Education
- Entertainment
- Games
- Health
- Home/Real Estate
- Horoscopes
- Lifestyle
- Money/Investing
- News
- People/Chat
- Shopping
- Sports
- Travel

Excite has put considerable effort into organizing each of the channels in a way uniquely useful to that topic, so it is difficult to generalize about the structure of the pages within channels.

The channel page shown in Figure 3.4 (see page 82) is about as typical as any. Here, under Education, the Universities and Colleges category was selected. On the left, under "Directories" we see where we are in the hierarchy, and the various levels can be instantly returned to through a mouse-click. Subsequent levels are shown, though you won't always find them on the left, nor always under the Web Directory heading. Other headings and positions are used in various channels. Most channels have links to chat rooms and message boards related to the topic of the channel. Many channels also have a section providing headlines and other news relevant to the channel topic.

Examples of levels and sublevels are:

Lifestyle
  Fifty Plus

Health

Travel

Business Travel

Hotel Reservations

Hotel Chains

A bottom level site listing page is shown in Figure 3.5. On the Right are Recommended Web Sites from the 25,000 sites that Excite has reviewed and recommended. Below that are additional sites.

SUMMARY OF EXCITE

As a mid-sized search engine, Excite is useful when you know there are more Web sites relevant to your topic than you need and you want to avoid wading through a tremendous amount of material. Since Excite has an automated thesaurus, it can retrieve useful records

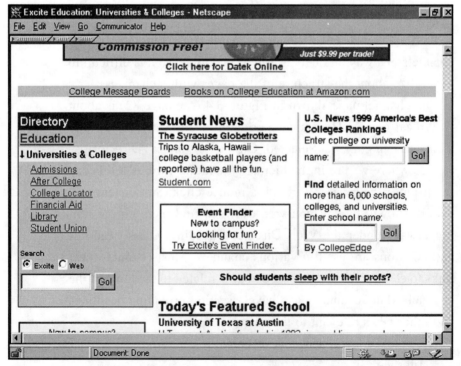

Figure 3.4 *The "Universities & Colleges" category (within the "Careers and Education" channel) in Excite's directory*

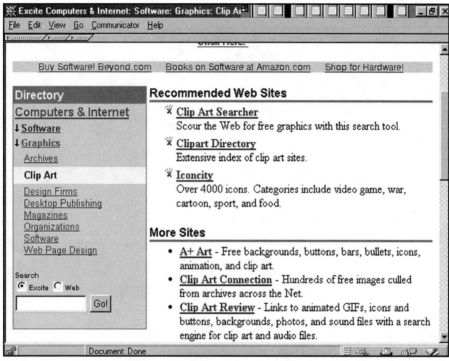

Figure 3.5   A bottom-level site listing in Excite's directory

without your having to put too much effort into planning the search. Since it has full Boolean capabilities, you can also do a more sophisticated search. If you are doing an exhaustive search, try Excite along with a couple of the larger engines. There is a good chance Excite will retrieve some additional relevant items.

For the serious searcher, Excite's greatest strength lies in its news resources—especially NewsTracker, which provides an excellent free news clipping service. If you have a topic on which you'd like to keep up-to-date, try this out. For those of you who are providing information support to other Web users, consider telling them about Excite's personalizable home page (but have them add a couple of other search engines in the Links section of the page). The kind of benefits this provides are comparable to what organizations had to pay thousands of dollars for just a few years ago.

CHAPTER 4

HotBot
www.hotbot.com

OVERVIEW

HotBot offers a variety of search options and presents most of them clearly on its home page. The advanced version presents more choices, including additional date-searching, location, and media type options, as well as a unique "top level" page designation. Serious searchers may want to bookmark the advanced page, rather than HotBot's home page. In addition to full Boolean, HotBot allows easy searching by media type (audio, video, etc.), domain, date, etc. Benchmarking shows that HotBot occasionally retrieves a larger number of sites than its competitors. The combination of a full range of search options and the fact that the available options

Strengths 👍	Weaknesses 👎
• Very large database • Broad range of search functionality • Extensive, easy, field searching • Clear presentation of options • Case-sensitive • Truncation and optional word stemming	• Has stop words

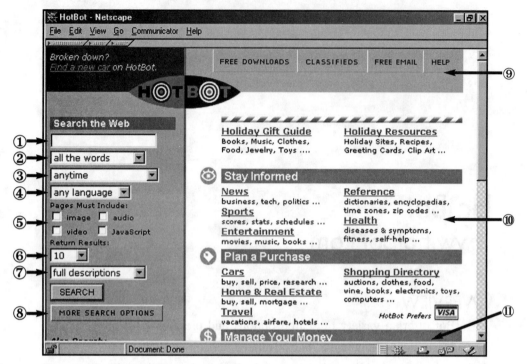

Figure 4.1   The HotBot home page

Search Options Displayed on HotBot's Home Page (Simple Version)

① **Query Box**

② **Look for:**
  - all the words
  - any of the words
  - the exact phrase
  - the page title
  - the person
  - links to this URL
  - Boolean phrase

③ **Date:** Anytime, in the last week, etc.

④ **Language:**
  - any language
  - Dutch
  - English
  - Finnish
  - French
  - German
  - Italian
  - Portuguese
  - Spanish
  - Swedish

⑤ **Media:**
  - Image
  - Audio
  - Video
  - Javascript

⑥ **Number of results per page:** 10, 25, 50, 100 records

⑦ **Format:**
  - full description
  - brief descriptions
  - URLs only

⑧ **More Search Options button:** (to get to HotBot's advanced version)

⑨ **Add-Ons and Help:** Shareware, Classifieds, Email

⑩ **Channels and Directory:** Includes links to HotBot's version of LookSmart
   (Below the area shown in the figure):

⑪ **Also Search:** Usenet, phone directories, and other add-ons.

are clearly presented make HotBot a good choice for both the frequent and occasional searcher.

HotBot has indexed about 110 million Web pages.

WHAT HAPPENS BEHIND THE SCENES

If terms are entered with no qualifiers or connectors, HotBot will AND all of the terms. Documents that match the search criteria are scored based on the following factors:

- Word frequency in document
- Occurrence of search words in the title
- Occurrence of search words as keywords—terms in metatags contribute more to the score than text words, but less than title words
- Document length—a specific number of occurrences in a short document rank higher than the same number of terms in a long document
- Anti-spamming—steps taken by HotBot to counter the tricks used by Web writers to cause a document to receive an artificially high score when examined by search engines. An example would be using a word hundreds of times in a document. If HotBot identifies spamming, it lowers the score.

HotBot has a list of stop words that are not indexed. At one point this list was quite long and included some valuable words such as "HTML" and "Web." The list now seems to be smaller and presents less of a problem for searchers.

Through an alliance with Direct Hit, Inc., HotBot also provides a very different alternative retrieval method for some searches that retrieve an extremely large set of results. On results pages for such searches (e.g., some single-word searches) you are given the option to "Get the Top 10 Most Visited Sites for..." When you click on that, HotBot then returns the ten pages that, in previous searches on the topic, other users have most frequently chosen to view. For some searches where "popularity" of a page may be a good indicator of usefulness, this can work very well.

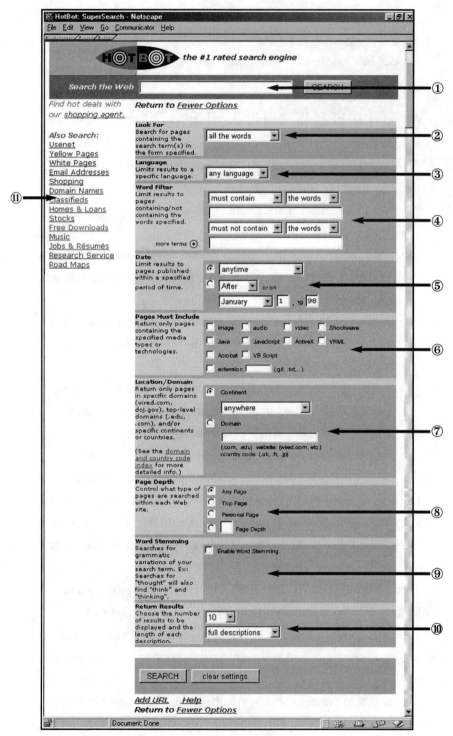

Figure 4.2 HotBot's advanced "More Search Options" page

HotBot Advanced Version Features
① **Query box:**
② **Look for:**
   - all the words
   - any of the words
   - the exact phrase
   - the page title
   - the person
   - links to this URL
   - Boolean phrase
③ **Language:**
   - any language
   - Dutch
   - English
   - Finnish
   - French
   - German
   - Italian
   - Portuguese
   - Spanish
   - Swedish
④ **Word filters:**
   - must contain
   - the word
   - should contain
   - the phrase
   - must not contain
   - the person
⑤ **Date:**
   - Option of specifying "anytime," "in the last week," etc.
   - After or before a specific date
⑥ **Media or types of technologies:**
   - Acrobat
   - Audio
   - ActiveX
   - Image
   - Java
   - JavaScript
   - Shockwave
   - VBScript
   - Video
   - VRML
   - Extensions (.gif, etc.)
⑦ **Location/Domain:**
   - Domain (.edu, .com, etc.—period is optional) *or* URL
   - Can choose a continent (as in the home page mode)
⑧ **Page depth:**
   - Any page (default)
   - Top page
   - You can specify how many pages "deep" you want to go (actually specifies how many directory levels of the URL are permitted).
⑨ **Word Stemming**—If you want to truncate words yourself, don't choose this.
⑩ **Return Results:**
   Format:
   - URLs only
   - full descriptions
   - brief descriptions
⑪ **Number of results per page:** 10, 25, 50, 100 records
   Also Search: Usenet, phone directories, and other add-ons

HotBot's Search Features: Advanced and Home Page Versions

One of HotBot's earlier advantages was that it provided its entire range of options in a single interface. In September 1997, they abolished this aspect of simplicity by offering two versions, the home page version and an advanced "More Search Options" version. To get to the advanced version, click the "More Search Options" button on the home page.

Boolean Logic

In either version of HotBot, if you want to use Boolean operators (AND, OR, NOT) you must choose the "Boolean phrase" option in the query box. If you do not, the operators you enter will be ignored.

- For AND, a more simplistic and less flexible approach is to use the "all the words" option in the "Look for" window. With this, an AND is applied to all the words entered.
- By using "any of the words," an OR is applied to all the words you enter
- On the advanced search page, by using the "must not contain" choice in the word filter windows a NOT is applied

Experienced searchers (in this case, anyone who has searched for more than an hour!) are advised to simply choose Boolean expression in the second box and use the following:

AND
OR
NOT
( )

Example:

(merger OR mergers) AND telecommunications NOT TCI

Truncation

*   HotBot provides both user-controlled truncation and the option of automatic word-stemming. In both versions of HotBot, to truncate, use the asterisk.

In the advanced version, you have the option of using automatic word stemming by clicking on the "Enable Word Stemming" box. When you do so, HotBot will retrieve some grammatical variations, e.g., "seek" will retrieve "seeking," etc.

If you wish to use stemming in a Boolean expression, do not click to "Enable Word Stemming" box. You must put the "stem:" prefix in front of the word.

Example: stem:appendectomy AND stem:complications

Stemming and truncation cannot be used together. In most cases, it will be simpler and probably more effective just to stick to truncation.

Phrases

Phrases can be searched either by entering the phrase and choosing "the phrase" as the type of search in the "Look for" window, or by using quotation marks around the phrase. Other than exact phrases, proximity searching is not available.

Example: "circuit boards"

Name Searching and Case-Sensitivity

When searching for a person's name in the "Look for" box, choose "the person" (however, so that you can copy and paste your entry most effectively into other search engines, capitalize the name appropriately). When you specify "the person," HotBot automatically searches for the inverted form as well as the normal form of the name.

Example: Winston Churchill will retrieve:
Winston Churchill and Churchill, Winston.

HotBot is case sensitive and will distinguish between "Green" and "green."

Field Searching

HotBot offers one of the best collections of searchable fields of all Web search engines. Fields are searched as shown in Table 4.1 (see page 92).

In addition to searching fields by making use of the checkboxes, radio buttons, and text boxes presented on its interface, HotBot offers the option of searching fields as part of your entry of terms in the query box, using what HotBot refers to as "meta words." These are entered using either "all the words" or "the Boolean phrase" in the "Look for" box. The list below shows the syntax for searching this way. The most significant options are covered by the boxes on the search page (and by using those boxes you don't have to worry about syntax). The truly obsessive searcher can use the following examples (see HotBot's HELP for details). The ones in bold are options not available in the panels (i.e., to use them they must be entered as meta words).

Table 4.1   Field Searching with HotBot
In the home page version, all options are located just below the main query box. For the advanced version, go to the area indicated in the "To search, use" column.

Field	To search, use:	HotBot Version:	Options/Examples
Date	Date panel	both	"in last week" "in last 2 weeks" "in last month" "in last 3 months" "in last 6 months" "in last year" "in last 2 years"
		Advanced	all of the above plus: (before or after) user-specified date
Title	"Look for" Panel	both	"the page title"
Language	Language Panel	both	English French, etc.
Domain	Location/Domain Panel	Advanced	user-specified (.edu, .com, .mil, net, etc.)
URL	Location/Domain Panel	Advanced	ford.com fleet.ford.com (up to three levels) (must have a term in the query box also)
Continent	Location/Domain Panel	Advanced	North America (.com) North America (.net) Europe, etc.
Media Type	"Page Must Include" Panel	both	image, audio, video, JavaScript
		Advanced	above plus VBScript Acrobat, Shockwave, ActiveX, Java, VRML .gif, etc. (user specified)
Page Depth	Page Depth Panel	Advanced	Any page (default) Top Page Page depth (user specified) Personal Pages
Links to URL	"Look for" Panel	both	"links to this URL"

HotBot Meta Words:

title:[term]	newsgroup:[name]
domain:[name]	depth:[number]
linkdomain:[name]	linkext:[extension]
scriptlanguage:[language]	feature:[name]
feature:embed	**feature:script**
feature:applet	feature:activex
feature:audio	feature:video
feature:shockwave	feature:acrobat
feature:frame	**feature:table**
feature:form	feature:vrml
feature:image	

HotBot Date Meta Words:

after:[day]/[month]/[year]
before:[day]/[month]/[year]
within:number/unit

Example: Vienna AND Virginia AND feature:frame

Caution: Some "meta words" do not always work the way HotBot documentation claims.

OUTPUT

HotBot will display up to 1000 results. Results are reported as:

asphalt AND cemex: 18 matches

Full Descriptions

3. CEMEX USA - Texas

Texas Sunbelt Asphalt & Materials operates two asphalt plants in Houston, Texas and a major limestone quarry in New Braunfels Texas. 5303 Navigation Houston, TX 77011 Ph: (713) 926-4461 Fx: (713) 926-9311 Sunbelt Cement produces about one million...

99% http://www.cemexusa.com/texas.htm

See results from this site only.

Brief Descriptions

3. 🖵   CEMEX USA - Texas

Texas Sunbelt Asphalt & Materials operates two asphalt plants in Houston, Texas and a major limestone quarry in New Braunfels Texas. 5303 Navigation Houston, TX 77011 Ph: (713) 926-4461 Fx: (713) 926-9311 Sunbelt Cement produces about one million...
See results from this site only.

URLs Only:

3. 🖵

http://www.cemexusa.com/texas.htm   **99%**
See results from this site only.

The percentage figure shown in records is HotBot's estimate of relevance for that record.

HotBot gives just one result per site. To see all the individual pages from a particular site, click on the "**See results from this site only**" link.

As mentioned earlier, HotBot has an alliance with Direct Hit for use of the latter's "popularity engine." For searches that are common enough, on results pages you will be given the option of the "**Top 10 Most Visited Sites**" for your topic. Clicking on this will lead to sites identified by Direct Hit as those records that were most frequently chosen (clicked on) by other users when they performed that search. This can be very useful when you are searching for something that is likely to yield a lot of records and you need just one or two good items.

By clicking on the 🖵 symbol in a record, the page will be opened in a new separate browser window. This makes it easier in some cases to return to the original search. By opening a page in a separate window, you retain immediate access to both your original search results and the pages you select from those results. (If you use either Netscape or Internet Explorer as your browser, you can do this in any of the search engines by holding your cursor over the link, clicking on the right mouse button, and choosing "**Open in New Window**." If you are on a Mac, hold down your button for a second.)

To enable you to easily modify your searches, on results pages HotBot presents the basic search options, with your original query in the query box. There is also a small checkbox allowing you to specify that your revised search be done just within the results already retrieved. Though the idea is clear, the real effect is not. If you modify the query in the query box, the new search seems to be done independently of whether you checked the "within these results" box.

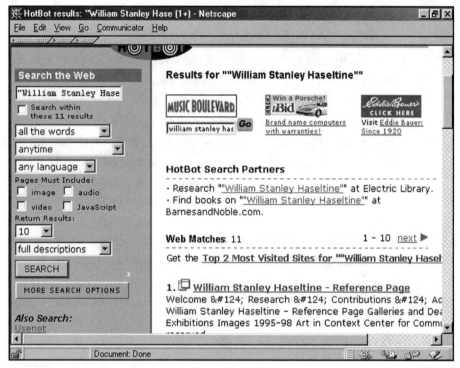

Figure 4.3   A HotBot results page

SPECIAL OPTIONS

Links to This URL

The "Links to this URL" search option (also available in AltaVista and Infoseek) provides an interesting way to locate pages related to your search topic. Analogous to the citation searching pioneered commercially by Eugene Garfield of the Institute for Scientific Information in the 1960s, by finding pages that link to a particular page you may be able to identify some relevant pages that you might not find using ordinary search techniques. For example, if you have done a search on evidential breath analysis and found a page that exactly addresses what you are looking for, it might be useful to look at pages that link to that page. Also, for company intelligence, it can be useful to find pages linking to the company of interest.

Page Depth

By using the Page Depth option on HotBot's Advanced page, you can specify that you want just the top level page of a site, or specify how far down in the hierarchy of a site's pages you are willing to go. One application of this would be looking for a company's home page. If, for example, you are looking for the compan, Biogen, specify Biogen as a title word and click on Top Page. It may take you directly to what you want without having to deal with over 100 other pages. (This, however, is one of those features that doesn't always work.)

Adult Content Filter

Check HotBot for the ability to filter out "adult content," a feature that was about to be implemented as this book was going to press.

ADD-ONS

Links to Specialized Searches

Specialized search links are found on the left of HotBot's main page. Note that most of these sites and databases are searched using search engines other than HotBot's. The specialized search links include:

- Usenet—Search of discussion groups, powered by Deja News
- Yellow Pages—Uses Big Yellow to search 16 million U.S. businesses
- White Pages—Uses Big Yellow to search 100 million U.S. residences
- Email Addresses—Uses Big Yellow to search 15 million email addresses
- Shopping—HotBot's shopping directory and shopping search engine (searchable by category, price, and keyword)

- Domain Names—Uses Web Sitez to search for domain names
- Classifieds—Searchable by category, not query
- Homes & Loans—Listings of properties for sale and mortgage rates
- Stocks—Get quotes, graphs, indexes, etc. Powered by Stock Point
- Free Downloads—Searches TUCOWS' collection of Internet-related software
- Music—Link to the Music Boulevard online music store
- Jobs & Resumes—A collection of job-related links by The Career Builder Network
- Research Service—Provides a link to the Electric Library's subscription service for magazines, maps, books & reports, newspapers & newswires, transcripts, and pictures
- Road Maps—For road maps and driving directions

HOTBOT'S DIRECTORY—LOOKSMART

Overview of LookSmart on HotBot

HotBot offers a classified directory of over 600,000 pages through a partnership with LookSmart (which is also available directly at http://looksmart.com). To get to the directory through HotBot, click on the appropriate subject category under the collection of channels heading on the right side of HotBot's home page. (see Figure 4.1 on page 86). In HotBot's Advanced version, to get to the directory, you must return to HotBot's home page by clicking the Return to Fewer Options link. (AltaVista has also partnered with LookSmart and is using the same directory. For the reader's convenience and because of differences in the implementation, LookSmart is discussed here and also in the chapter on AltaVista.)

HotBot, in its aim to be a "Web portal" rather than just a search engine, has created a collection of channels that it has organized into four categories: Stay Informed, Plan a Purchase, Manage Your Money, and Use Technology. Each of these categories contains from three to five channels. Embedded in the main pages for each of these channels you may find a section for "More Sites" (for example, "More Travel Sites"). Whether you regard it a matter of integrated, embedded, or hidden, this is where you get to LookSmart through HotBot.

Searchability of LookSmart on Hotbot

The LookSmart Directory is searchable on HotBot, that is, you can enter a term and search the contents of the directory for that term. Strangely, though, this is possible only when you have browsed all the way down to the bottom of the hierarchy and have arrived at a page with site listings. Up until that point, the directory is browsable but not searchable. There are some fairly minor exceptions to this lack of searchability; in a few places in the hierarchy there are searchable subcategories such as the Destinations search in the Travel category.

Structure of LookSmart on Hotbot

LookSmart's thirteen main categories, shown in Figure 4.4, contain over 24,000 subcategories and 600,000 pages. For most of the categories, there are three or four additional levels of hierarchy.

In Figure 4.4, the Health & Fitness category was selected, then within that, the Drugs & Medicines category. Clicking on any of the subcategories on the right may lead either to additional subcategories or to a list of actual sites.

LookSmart's top levels are:

- Automotive
- Business & Finance
- Computers & Internet
- Entertainment & Media
- Health & Fitness
- Hobbies & Interests
- Home & Family
- People & Chat
- Reference & Education
- Shopping & Services

Figure 4.4   A HotBot directory page, showing examples of subcategories

- Society & Politics
- Sports & Recreation
- Travel & Vacations

Examples of levels and sublevels are:

Travel & Vacations
   Europe
      Britain & Ireland
         Culture & Amusements
         Historic Sites
Hobbies & Interests
   Genealogy & Heraldry
      Heraldry
      Arms

As shown in Figure 4.5 (see page 100), preceding the listing of sites is a summary line indicating where you are in the classification hierarchy.

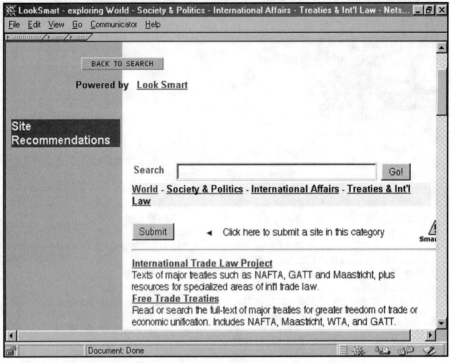

Figure 4.5   A HotBot directory page, showing final-level site listings

You can return to a level of your choice by clicking on the appropriate place in this summary line. World refers toLookSmart's top level.

SUMMARY OF HOTBOT

For the serious searcher, HotBot is without a doubt at or near the top when size, functionality, quality of retrieval, and ease of use are considered. It has been running a close race with AltaVista in terms of size and has recently added to its arsenal of searching features. Just as important, in contrast to its major competitor, AltaVista, and similar to its newest competitor, Northern Light, the options available to the searcher are clearly laid out, so the user knows what is possible and the options can easily be utilized. Because of this, HotBot is a good choice not just for the frequent searcher, but for the less frequent searcher. For any search where exhaustiveness is required, HotBot should be one of the engines searched.

Infoseek
www.infoseek.com

OVERVIEW

Infoseek offers a fairly full range of options including most of the features one might expect in a search engine: relevance ranking, Boolean (minimal), phrase, name, and field searching. In addition, it provides a directory. Infoseek has an advanced version that provides more choices in terms of what is to be searched and a much more explicit presentation of search options (though the actual search functionality is about the same as in the home page version). A useful feature is the ability to narrow results by modifying a set of retrieved records. Infoseek is targeting the "average, nontechnical consumer." It

Strengths	Weaknesses
• Effective integration of directory and Web searching • Can narrow results • Subject classification (top level searchable) • No stop words • Can search diacritics • Automatic truncation • Suggests related directory categories • Country-specific versions	• Minimal Boolean • Numbers of items retrieved tend to be low

Figure 5.1   The Infoseek home page

Main Options Displayed on Infoseek's Home Page

① **Links to:**

- Stocks
- News
- Maps
- Free Web Page
- UPS Tracking
- People Finder
- Yellow Pages
- Chat
- Shareware
- Company Capsules

② **Link to Advanced Search**

③ **Query Box**

④ **Choice of Searching:**

- Web
- News
- Companies
- Usenet

⑤ **Topics Directory** (Channels)

⑥ **Headlines**

⑦ **Not Shown Above** (found on bottom portion of the home page):

- Links to Worldwide Infoseek: ("Brasil, Danmark, Deutschland, en español, France, Italia, Japan, Nederland, Sverige, United Kingdom")
- Help, etc.

is one of the most "global/local" of the services, with individualized sites for 12 countries plus a site for Spanish-speaking users. Infoseek is estimated to have indexed about 30 million Web pages.

In contrast to the home page version, Infoseek's Advanced Search page provides a much more explicit presentation of the search options available, plus more control over output (format and number of records per page). In the home page version virtually all of the same search features are available, but the user must know to use **+word** and **-word** (for Boolean expressions) and field prefixes in order to take advantage of these options. In addition to clearly laying out the user's options, the advanced version provides the choice of searching just Infoseek's directory—an option not available in the home page version.

To get to the Advanced Search (see Figure 5.2 on page 104) version from the home page, click on the Advanced Search link to the right of the query box.

WHAT HAPPENS BEHIND THE SCENES

In 1998, Infoseek introduced its Extra Search Precision (ESP) software that is designed to deal with searches on very general topics, particularly searches that consist of only one or two words. It does this based on previous users' searches on these topics. Things to remember about what Infoseek does with queries are as follows:

- When a list of terms is entered without qualifiers, the system defaults to an OR, unless the words are capitalized, in which case the words are searched as a phrase.
- Infoseek indexes (searches) the full text of the page.
- Infoseek has no stop words, which is important if you need to search a common word. 👍
- Searching is case sensitive (with a few apparent exceptions). 👍
- Along with the use of ESP, Infoseek sorts search results based on a "scoring" algorithm that looks at whether the query terms (words or phrases) are found in the title or near the beginning of the document, at how many of the query terms are found, and at whether a query term is one that is assigned a higher "weight" because it is a relatively uncommon term.

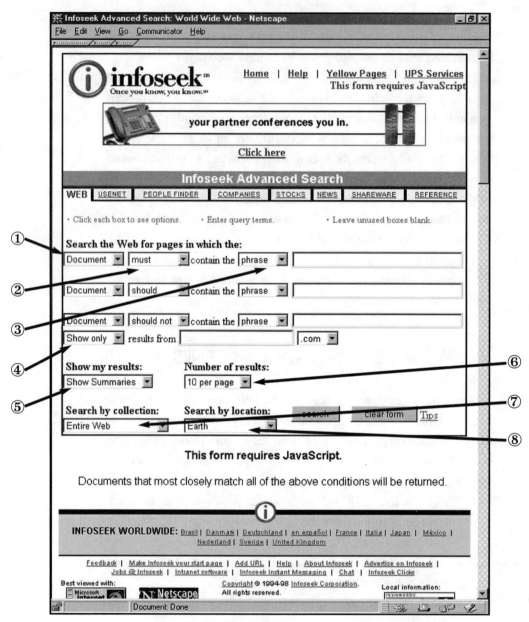

Figure 5.2   Infoseek's Advanced Search page

Main Options Displayed on Infoseek's Advanced Search Page

① **Window allowing choice of fields to be searched:**

- Document—for searching all fields

- Title—for searching for those pages with the selected term(s) in the title

- • URL—for searching just within pages that are a part of a particular URL
- • Hyperlink—for finding pages that link to a particular page

② **Window specifying that the query terms:**
- • should [be present] (equivalent to a Boolean OR)
- • must [be present] (equivalent to a Boolean AND)
- • should not [be present] (equivalent to a Boolean NOT)

③ Window specifying that the query terms be searched as a phrase, a name, or words

④ Windows to "show only" or "exclude" results from a particular domain name and extension. Note that if the results from window is left blank, this line does not have any effect.

⑤ "Show my results" window, allowing you to specify output format, either with or without summaries

⑥ "Number of results" window, allowing a choice of 10,20,25 or 50 results per page

⑦ **"Search by Collection" choice, specifying a search of:** 👍
- • Infoseek's entire Web index
- • all Infoseek channels (Infoseek's entire directory)
- • specific Infoseek channels (a search of particular categories within the directory)

⑧ "Search by location" window, allowing specification of country or continent of origin for pages ("Earth" for all pages)

SEARCH FEATURES: HOME PAGE VERSION & ADVANCED VERSION

Boolean Logic

Its failure to provide a robust Boolean search capability is one of Infoseek's weakest points. Though Infoseek offers the equivalent of an AND, a NOT, and an implied OR, the lack of nesting (parentheses) capability means that sophisticated Boolean expressions cannot be specified. 👎

Home Page Version

Infoseek's Home Page version provides the following as its Boolean options:

+word   for AND: put a plus sign (+) in front of the term
-word   for NOT: put a minus sign (-) in front of the term
             Example: +Cuba +tourism

| You can use a pipe to search within a certain set of retrieved pages.

Note that the following are all "logically" equivalent and retrieve the same records. Although purportedly there is a difference in how the relevance ranking is calculated among these three approaches, the actual effect in terms of which records are displayed first is not easily discerned.

+television +commercials

television | commercials

commercials | television

Advanced Search Version

The same Boolean functions are available in Infoseek's Advanced Search version as in its home page version, but they are more clearly presented in the Advanced version by means of a series of windows (see Figure 5.2 on pages 104-105).

Truncation

Truncation in both Infoseek versions is done automatically, and it finds variants such as "mice" when "mouse" is searched. There is no way to override the automatic truncation. 👍

Phrase Searching

Home Page Version

" "   Use double quotation marks.

Advanced Search Version

Choose "phrase" in the appropriate window (see Figure 5.2 on pages 104-105).

In both versions, Infoseek searches "across spaces." For instance, a search for "The Who" found "Thew-Ho Yik's Home Page" (as well as relevant records).

Name Searching

To search for proper names in both the home page and advanced versions, capitalize the first letter of each name.

In the home page version, use commas to separate names and titles, for instance:

Example: George Bush, Jimmy Carter

In the Advanced Search version, choose "**name**" in the "**contain the**" window(s).

Infoseek uses capitalization to identify names, but based on the "**Thew-Ho**" example above, Infoseek does not seem to be completely case-sensitive, which seems to at least somewhat negate the reliability of this approach with Infoseek.

No matter which engine you are using, capitalize the first letters of proper names and put them in quotes, so they can be easily copied and pasted when you want to repeat the search in another engine.

Field Searching

Home Page Version

Title, URL, site, links, and "alternate text" for images are searchable using the following syntax:

Examples: title:"used cars"
url:netscape
site:travelocity.com
link:infoseek.com (this will find
    pages that link to Infoseek)
alt:porsche

You can use combinations of the above for better precision. For instance, for sites mentioning **Cameroon** that only appear on the Travelocity Web site:

> *Example*: +site:travelocity.com +Cameroon

Advanced Search Version

In the first set of windows, under "Search the Web pages in which the...," choose "title," "URL," or "hyperlink."

The domain name and file extension (.com, etc.) portions of a URL are also specifiable in the "results from" and "search by location" windows.

OUTPUT

On results pages, Infoseek shows the following:

- Recommended—Places (within Infoseek Channels) that Infoseek's search technology identifies as "Recommended" based on what others have looked for. This shows up in relatively few searches and the relevance is sometimes obscure.
- Directory Topics—Subject headings from Infoseek's directory that contain your search terms. This is a very useful and effective integration of Infoseek's directory benefits into Web searching. 👍
- Web Results—From the full Infoseek Web database.

Infoseek reports the results of searches as follows:

> Your search for +Thailand +history resulted in:
>
> 2 Recommended Links
>
> 14 Directory Topics
>
> 346 Web Search Results

In the home page version, you cannot specify the format or number of records to be displayed. In the Advanced Search version you can specify both (see Figure 5.2 on pages 104-105).

On any results page you can elect to "Hide Summaries" to get a shorter format. Results from the same site are grouped under a single entry. To see the other matching records from that site, click the "Ungroup these results" link at the top of the results list.

Results are listed by their relevance score (the percent number shown in each record). Very conveniently, Infoseek also gives you the option to "Sort by Date."

Infoseek also provides an option to "Find similiar pages."

Default Record Format:
Israel's Peace Process: Selected Reference Documents
Israel's Ministry of Foreign Affairs provides this collection of historical documents, treaties and accords relating to attempts at peace between Israel and her neighbors.
100% Date: **1 Nov 1998**, Size 6.5K, http://www.israel.org/peace/basicref.html
Find similiar pages | Grouped results from www.israel.org

"Hide Summaries" format:
Israel's Peace Process: Selected Reference Documents   100% (Size 6.5K)
Find similiar pages | Grouped results from www.israel.org

Figure 5.3   An Infoseek results page, showing directory topics and Web results

SPECIAL OPTIONS

Infoseek Express

This is a free downloadable metasearch program that provides searching of multiple search engines, including most of the major engines (AltaVista, Excite, HotBot, Infoseek, Lycos, plus WebCrawler and Yahoo!). It provides nicely integrated results, plus additional features such as elimination of duplicates and highlighting of search terms in results. As with most other metasearch engines (see Chapter 10), it does not carry any sophisticated syntax such Boolean or field searching over into the target engines. It does allow for words, phrases, and a choice of either OR or AND.

Reviewed Web Site Topics

For some searches, on results pages, Infoseek will provide links to related categories from Infoseek directory. These are shown above the list of matching sites. Clicking on one of the categories will lead to sites from the directory. For very common searches (e.g., "baseball"), Infoseek also provides a list of "Recommended" sites.

Searching Within a Topic Area

Infoseek allows you to search within a specific classification (channel). However, this is only available at the top level of the classification scheme, for example, within the business category.

Searching Diacritics

You can search using diacritical marks. For example: résumé vs. resume, cinéma vs. cinema, etc.

Ability to Narrow Results

On results pages, you are given the option of modifying your search by adding other terms and having the modification apply only to your prior search results. This feature, which allows you to narrow your results, can be extremely useful. In providing this feature, Infoseek comes as close as any of the other search engines to allowing you to work with results "sets."

ADD-ONS

The following options are listed at the top of the home page:

- Stocks—Quotes, price history, market snapshots, personal portfolios, etc.
- News—Leads to the Infoseek News Channel, which provides access to newswires, including Business Wire, PR Newswire and Reuters, and other national and international news sources including the Chicago Tribune, CNN, Los Angeles Times, MSNBC, Nando.net, The New York Times, San Jose Mercury News, USA TODAY, and the Washington Post
- Maps—Provides an Infoseek-branded version of MapQuest
- People Finder—A collection of phone, email, and other directories powered by AnyWho, Microsoft Sidewalk, and other services
- Yellow Pages—A directory of U.S. businesses from Microsoft
- UPS Tracking
- Chat—from WBS (WebChat Broadcasting System)
- Free Web Page—from WBS
- Shareware—Infoseek's shareware directory
- Company Capsules—Infoseek's index of, and link to, profiles from Hoovers Online
- "More"—A reference collection containing maps (from MapQuest), a dictionary, thesaurus, etc.

The following options are found in the pull-down window beneath the query box and offer alternative types of searching:

- News—Searches newswires

    (Note that this differs from the "News" option at the top of the Infoseek home page in that a search entered here will be done on PR Newswire, Businesswire, and Reuters. The option at the top of the home page takes you directly to the Infoseek News Channel.)

- Company Capsules—Searches 13,500 companies from the Hoover's directory
- Newsgroups—For searches of newsgroup postings using Deja News

Other options, found at the bottom of the Infoseek home page, include:

- Links to Infoseek Worldwide ("Brasil, Danmark, Deutschland, en español, France, Italia, Japan, Nederland, Mexico, Sverige, United Kingdom") 👍
- Help

Other add-ons relevant to particular subject areas are found when various Channel pages are displayed.

INFOSEEK'S DIRECTORY

Overview of Infoseek's Directory

Infoseek's Directory contains over 500,000 pages, making it one of the largest of the search engine directories. The main Infoseek page contains the topic index, with broad categories such as Automotive, Business, and Entertainment. Infoseek's channels provide not just a classification of Web sites, but a number of channel-specific options such as searchable stock quotes, searchable product reviews, a currency converter, and searchable real estate listings.

Searchability of Infoseek's Directory

You can search within a topic area at the first level (only) for most of the channels. You can choose, for example, the business channel and limit your retrieval to only those records that are classified under "business." If you are looking for business aspects of pharmaceuticals, you may want to choose to search just in the business category to avoid the thousands of pages that deal with other aspects of the topic. Keep

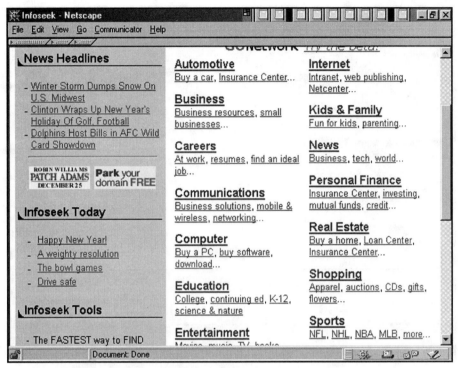

***Figure 5.4 Portion of the Infoseek home page showing directory
categories (channels)***

in mind that when searching any of the directories associated with a
search engine, you are searching only a small portion of the total number of pages indexed by the service. (This is not true of Yahoo! of
course, since technically Yahoo! itself is a directory rather than a search
engine. When you search Yahoo!, you are searching all of Yahoo!.)

When you have searched in an Infoseek category, the system provides the option of narrowing your search by searching in only those
pages just retrieved.

Structure of Infoseek's Directory

The contents of the Infoseek Directory are classified into the
following 18 channels:

- Automotive   • Business   • Careers
- Communications   • Computer   • Education

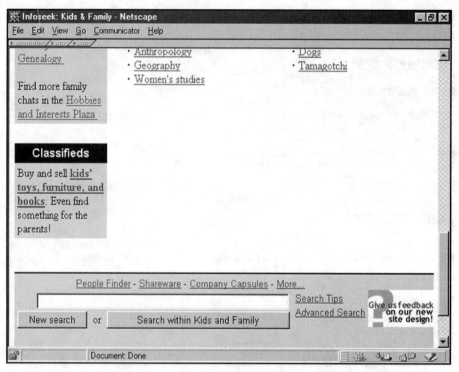

Figure 5.5   Infoseek first-level directory page, showing a search box that allows searching of the entire Web, or just within the current category

- Entertainment
- Internet
- Personal Finance
- Sports

- The Good Life
- Kids & Family
- Real Estate
- Travel

- Health
- News
- Shopping
- Women's

Within each of the main categories, Infoseek provides a selection of category-specific options, such as a car-buying guide in Automotive, "company capsules" in Business, etc.

Examples of levels and sublevels are:

Education
  Colleges & universities
    Continuing education
      Professional development
Business
  Int'l commerce
    Trade

> Law & regulations
> > U.S. export programs

Within each of the channels, for the actual directory subcategories, look for the "topics" listing on the left of the page. Infoseek provides a line toward the top of subcategory pages that lets you know where you are.

> *Example:* Personal Finance > Banking > Banking online
> > Online banking software

You can click on any of the levels shown and return immediately to that level.

Special Features of Infoseek's Directory

All sites listed in Infoseek's directory have been reviewed, and the reviewer's opinion is indicated by the presence of either one, two, or three red stars by the entry for the site.

Most channels have a channel-specific news feature, with current headlines from a variety of news sources.

SUMMARY OF INFOSEEK

Infoseek is a respectable, mid-sized service that—like Lycos—is a good choice when you don't want to deal with a large number of sites. It generally retrieves far fewer pages than AltaVista, HotBot, or Northern Light. Infoseek has a moderate level of search functionality, but the lack of full Boolean capabilities is a drawback for some searches. If an exhaustive search is your aim, Infoseek would probably not be your first stop, but should probably be included among your list of engines to search, since it may find a few the others miss. Its large directory would be another reason for stopping by. As with the other mid-sized services, try Infoseek at least occasionally—you are likely to see it continue to change and grow in order to keep pace with the competition.

CHAPTER 6

Lycos
www.lycos.com

OVERVIEW

Lycos provides two levels of searching. The Lycos home page version has minimal search features (+word, -word, " "). The second level, Lycos Pro Search, provides more options, though the availability of Lycos' most powerful features, full Boolean and proximity, is obscured. The user must read the documentation to find that Lycos has full Boolean and the Web's largest collection of proximity connectors. In Lycos Pro Search, the user is also given extensive control over the relevance weighting. For users who need to locate images or audio files, Lycos makes it very easy.

Lycos' documentation is extensive but occasionally weak. With all the emphasis the documentation gives to Boolean and proximity,

Strengths	Weaknesses
• User control of relevance ranking • Largest collection of proximity operators • Offers best option for name searching (NEAR/2) • Ability to narrow results • Very effective picture and sound searching	• Boolean option not obvious • Major omissions in documentation • No truncation • Numbers of items retrieved are low

it does not tell which search window choice (for instance, "all the words") must be used to apply the Boolean (and there is no window choice that says "Boolean"). In addition, the documentation is not updated quickly when changes are made in the interface.

Lycos claims to have indexed about 35 million Web pages.

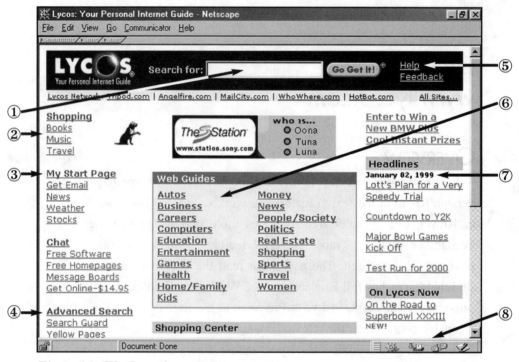

Figure 6.1   The Lycos home page

Main Options Displayed on Lycos' Home Page

① **Query box**: Minimal Boolean can be used:
  - **+word** To AND a term, use a plus sign directly in front of the word.
  - **-word** To NOT a term, use a minus sign directly in front of the word.
② **Add-ons:** Shopping, weather, news, stocks, etc.
③ Link to **Personalization options** ("My Start Page")
④ Link to **Advanced Search Mode** (Lycos Pro Search)
⑤ **Help link**
⑥ **Channels/Directory** (Web Guides)
⑦ **Headline News**
⑧ (At bottom of screen, not shown in the above figure):
  - **Country-specific versions of Lycos**

THE TWO VERSIONS OF LYCOS

The difference between the Lycos Home Page version and Lycos' advanced version, Lycos Pro Search, is more pronounced than with most other search engines. The home page version has minimal search functionality, whereas Lycos Pro Search has full Boolean capabilities, good proximity operators, some field searching, and unique user-controlled revelance ranking.

WHAT HAPPENS BEHIND THE SCENES

Lycos claims to index every word on each page with the exception of some stopwords such as "the," "a," and "and." In simple search mode, when a string of terms is entered, all records resulting from an ANDing of terms are retrieved. Beyond the simplest (Lycos home) level, retrieval is controlled further by the user's application of Boolean, proximity, etc. The Lycos Pro Search options for weighting the relevance ranking factors give the user unique control over which items will appear first in the results list.

SEARCH FEATURES

Boolean

Lycos Home

+word   To AND a term, use a plus sign directly in front of the word.

-word   To NOT a term, use a minus sign directly in front of the word.

Lycos Pro Search

The same as for Lycos home (+word, -word), plus:

                    AND
                    OR
                    NOT
                    ( )

Example:

"New England" AND (lobster OR lobsters) NOT recipe

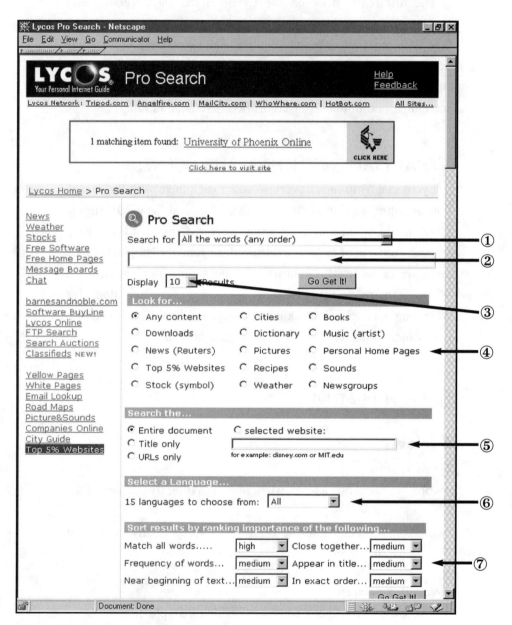

Figure 6.2 The Lycos Pro Search page

Main Options Displayed on the Lycos Pro Search Page
① **Search for:**
- All the words (any order)
- All the words (within 25 words, in order)
- All the words (in order)
- All the words (within 25 words, any order)
- All the words (adjacent any order)
- The exact phrase
- Natural language query

(Note that Lycos does not show the Boolean option. To use Boolean, use the default "All of the words")

② **Query Box**—You can use full Boolean and the Lycos proximity connectors (ADJ, NEAR, etc.)

③ **Display**—10, 20, 30, or 40 results per page

④ Choice of **which Lycos database** to search (or subset of the main Lycos Web database)
- Any content (the Web)
- Cities (Lycos City Guide)
- Books (Barnes & Noble)
- Downloads (ZDNet Software Library)
- American Heritage Dictionary
- Music (CD Now)
- News (Reuters)
- Pictures
- Personal Home Pages
- Top 5% Web sites
- Recipes
- Sounds
- Stock (by symbol)
- Weather
- Newsgroups

⑤ You can choose to **search**:
- the entire document (the default setting)
- title only
- URLs only
- a selected Web site

⑥ You can select to only retrieve sites in the following **languages**:
- English
- Danish
- Dutch
- French
- Finnish
- Gaelic
- German
- Icelandic
- Italian
- Norwegian
- Portuguese
- Slovenian
- Spanish
- Swedish
- Welsh

⑦ You have the option of **sorting** your results by ranking the importance of the following:
- Match all words
- Close together
- Frequency of words
- Appear in title
- Near beginning of text
- In exact order

You may weight the preceding options as "high," "medium," or "low." This implementation of a user-controlled ranking scheme is unique to Lycos among Web search engines.

Truncation

Truncation is not available in either version of Lycos.

Phrase/Proximity Searching

" "   Use double quotation marks to search on a phrase (available in both versions of Lycos)

Lycos Pro Search has the broadest range of proximity connectors of all major search engines. The following are available in Lycos Pro Search: 👍

• ADJ	Terms must be next to each other (either order)
• ADJ/n	Terms must be within n words of each other (either order)
• NEAR	Terms must be within 25 words of each other
• NEAR/n	Terms must be within n words of each other
• FAR	Terms must be at least 25 words apart
• FAR/n	Terms must be at least n words apart
• BEFORE	The first term you enter must appear before the second term, any distance apart
• OADJ, ONEAR	Applies specified order of terms
• OFAR	
• OADJ/n, etc.	Applies specified order, within a certain number words of each other

Example:

Scott NEAR/2 Fitzgerald AND "Great Gatsby"

Name Searching

Lycos is case-insensitive and cannot distinguish between "Frank" and "frank." To get the effect of name searching:

• In Lycos home, search using double quotes. You may want to capitalize the name, so you can copy and paste it into other engines.

Example:

"John M. Shalikashvili"

• In Lycos Pro Search, use **ADJ** for adjacency, or use **NEAR/2** to allow the words to be within two words of each other. This will allow for inverted or middle names. 👍

Examples:

Vladimir NEAR/2 Lenin

Revere NEAR/2 Paul

George NEAR/2 Bush

Field Searching

Using the list of options on the Lycos Pro Search page, Lycos provides the capability of searching either within the title or URL fields. However, titles must be searched by themselves, not as part of a longer search—i.e., you can specify that you want pages with "banking" in the title, but you cannot specify that you want "banking" in the title and AND it with other criteria.

For URLs, the user has the option of searching the entire URL or performing a search of terms within a particular site (URL). To search for specific pages within a URL, put your query terms in the query box (see Figure 6.2 on pages 120-121), then on the Lycos Pro Search page under "Search the:" click on the radio button for "selected Web sites" and enter the URL you want.

To search for all pages that are part of a particular URL, enter the URL itself in the query box, then click (under "Search the:") the radio button for "URLs only."

OUTPUT

Lycos does not report the number of items retrieved. If your results set happens to be less than 100, you can get an idea of the size by looking at the bottom of a results page to see how many additional pages are available to look at. With 10 sites per page, if you see the numbers 1 through 7 as possible pages you know you have 70-some answers.

Output results are conveniently arranged by Web site, with multiple pages from the same Web site being grouped together.

Though Lycos previously provided three format options, it now only provides one:

Chemical & Engineering News

Chemical & Engineering News, December 11, 1995 Copyright ©
1995 by the American Chemical Society. Chemical Industry
http://acsinfo.acs.org/hotartcl/cenear/951211/mex.html
Similiar pages | More pages from acsinfo.acs.org | acsinfo.acs.org

Clicking on "Similiar pages" in the record above will produce records that are similiar, but not necessarily from the same site. Clicking on "More pages from..." will yield other pages from that site and clicking on the URL (acsinfo.acs.org) will take you to that specific page.

At the top of results pages, if one or more of the terms in your query matches a subject heading in the Lycos directory, you will see the (clickable) subject heading(s) listed (even if your query contained a Boolean AND and only one of the words from your query was in a subject heading). Following that, Lycos presents a section entitled "Check These Out." By clicking on the appropriate entry, your search will be performed in one of the other databases available through Lycos, such as Barnes & Noble, the dictionary, news, etc. This is followed by the actual results of your search.

At the bottom of results pages (see Figure 6.4 on page 126), Lycos search options are presented. If you do your search in the Lycos home version, you'll see the query box plus the option of either performing a new search or "Search These Results." This ability to narrow your current results can be quite helpful in refining your search.

If you are in Lycos Pro Search you will see the query box and additional search options.

At the bottom of the results pages you will notice a link that carries your search over into HotBot. HotBot is a member of the Lycos "family," having been purchased by Lycos in 1998.

SPECIAL OPTIONS

Personalization

Lycos, like some other search engine services, allows you to personalize its home page. By clicking on "My Start Page," you can select which category of news headlines you would like to appear on the page and select local news by state. For stocks, you can select which stocks and/or indices you would like to see, and there is a link to a portfolio service where you can track your own portfolio. The entire portfolio will not appear on your personalized Lycos page, only the listing of stocks and current activity (not the total values for your own holdings).

The personalized page also provides a section for you to place your favorite links (bookmarks), local weather, sports scores, etc. The "Contacts" link leads to a personal address book, calendar, and reminders section.

Lycos does not provide a capability for current awareness searches, nor does it provide highly specialized news categories.

Pictures and Sounds

Other Web search engines allow searching for pictures (images) and sounds (audio), but Lycos is among the most straightforward and easy to use for these types of searches. In Lycos Pro Search, under the "Look for" section, you can choose Pictures or Sounds. When you search for an image and click on the items retrieved, Lycos takes you directly to the image, rather than to the page that contains the image. The "titles" of the records you retrieve are from the ALT (alternate text) tag in the HTML coding. (This is the "label" you see when you hold the cursor over an image on a page.)

ADD-ONS

The following add-ons are located primarily on the left of both the Lycos home and Pro Search screens:

- News (headlines, by category, with search capability)
- Weather (weather)
- Stocks (stock quotes and market news using News Alert—one of the best free Web services for this type of information)
- Free Software (Accesses the ZDNet Software Library)

Figure 6.3   A Lycos results page

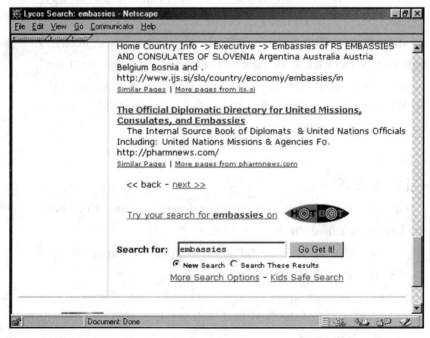

Figure 6.4   Bottom of a Lycos results page showing options for refining your current search or beginning a new search

- Free Home Pages (From Tripod.com and Angelfire)
- Message Boards (a variety of easy-to-use moderated message boards)
- Web Guides (subject directory to sites selected by Lycos)
- Personalize (allows you to personalize a news page)
- Chat (what you'd expect)
- Email (free email service)
- Top 5% Sites (contains reviews of selected Web sites)
- CityGuide (a guide to over 800 cities in the U.S., Canada, Europe, and Australia)
- Pictures and Sounds (graphics, photos, video and sound files)
- Barnes & Noble (their online bookstore)
- Classifieds (classified advertising)
- Companies Online (link to the D&B CompaniesOnline database)
- White Pages (phone, email, and other directories from WhoWhere and other sources)
- UPS Services (package tracking and guide to drop-off centers)
- Yellow Pages (GTE Superpages)
- Road Maps (custom maps and driving directions)
- Lycos Europe (nine country-specific versions of Lycos: Belgium, France, Germany, Italy, Netherlands, Spain, Sweden, Switzerland, United Kingdom)

Lycos also provides a feature called Search Guard, which screens out adult content. A user registers for the service, then clicks on a link on either the home page or results pages to activate it.

LYCOS' DIRECTORY (WEB GUIDES)

Overview

Lycos' directory is relatively small. Subcategories have additional featured sites and resources listings that lead to specialized features such as phone directories and road maps. Sites within the Web Guides are rated by users, and users of the directory can vote on the usefulness of a site they visit. These are tallied in order to assign the ranking used when the sites in a particular category are listed.

Searchability

Though a search box is provided on the first-level page for each category, it allows only a search of the entire Lycos database itself, not a search of the sites in the directory.

Structure of the Directory

Lycos' Web Guides are divided into 19 main categories:

- Autos
- Business
- Careers
- Computers
- Education
- Entertainment
- Games
- Health
- Home/Family
- Kids
- Money
- News
- People/Society
- Politics
- Real Estate
- Shopping
- Sports
- Travel
- Women

For each of these main categories there are generally three to five levels of hierarchy (most typically, three). As with most other directories provided by search engines, with Lycos Web Guides you are always shown where you are in a hierarchy and you can click on any level shown in order to return to that level.

Examples of levels and sublevels are:

Business
    Issues
        International Economy
Health
    Diseases
        Cardiovascular
            Endocarditis

Figure 6.5 A typical Lycos Web Guide page at a third level of a category

SUMMARY OF LYCOS

Lycos, with its medium-sized database, is an engine you might wish to start with if you expect a lot of material to be available on your topic and want to retrieve a manageable number of pages. Lycos should definitely be considered if you have a search that can benefit from the ability to specify how far apart you wish terms to be, since Lycos has the largest collection of proximity operators. Furthermore, Lycos is the only search engine that allows the user to manipulate relevance ranking. Lycos is a particularly good starting place for image or audio file searches.

The numbers of items retrieved using Lycos tend to be among the smallest of the major Web search engines, so don't expect it to retrieve much in addition to what you can find with the other engines.

CHAPTER 7

Northern Light
www.northernlight.com <u>or</u>
www.nlsearch.com

OVERVIEW

Northern Light's uniqueness lies in (1) its coverage of proprietary publications (Special Collection) as well as the Web, and, (2) its organization of results into customized folders. For the proprietary material, abstracts are provided free and the full text can be purchased by credit card or subscription. This material includes over 5,000 magazines, journals, books, newspapers, newsletters, pamphlets, and newswires. Both Northern Light's Web index and its proprietary collection cover all subject areas. When a search is done, Northern Light groups the results into "Custom Search Folders."

Strengths 👍	Weaknesses 👎
• Wide range of search functionality • Searches and provides full-text document delivery for proprietary information as well as general Web content • Analyzes and organizes results by "folders" • Unique, powerful field-searching capabilities	• Lack of proximity operators

These folders bring together those results that have common characteristics such as subject category, type of document, etc.

Northern Light now has a broad range of search functionality, including an excellent capability for searching by field. The Power Search version provides much the same functionality of the home page versions, but makes the various options more apparent by means of checkboxes and windows. With its proprietary information resources, Northern Light is not just a Web search service, but a bibliographic search service and a document delivery service as well.

Northern Light's database includes over 120 million Web pages and over 4 million proprietary articles.

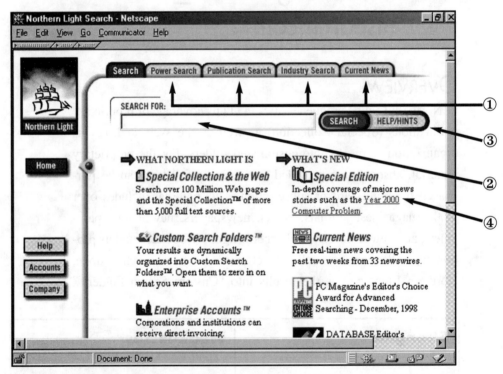

Figure 7.1   Northern Light home page

Northern Light Home Page Options

① **Links to**
- Power Search
- Current News Search
- Publication Search (to search by publication)
- Industry Search (to search by industry)

② Query Box

③ Help

④ Links to descriptions of Northern Light's special features

WHAT HAPPENS BEHIND THE SCENES

Northern Light indexes every word contained in a page and every page of a Web site, including metatags, but it does not weight metatag contents higher than other words. The text of proprietary documents is likewise fully indexed. Northern Light retains information on document source, type, subject, and language, which is used for the creation of the Custom Search Folders. As part of that process, Northern Light automatically classifies every document, using a controlled vocabulary "which recognizes several hundreds of thousands of concepts." If you have not specified an AND, OR, or NOT, Northern Light will retrieve those records that contain "most of the words in your search." Relevancy is calculated based on several factors, including occurrences of query terms and the presence of query terms in document titles. Results are listed according to that relevancy determination.

SEARCH FEATURES

Boolean

With Northern Light you can use the simplified Boolean:

+word	To AND a term, use a plus sign directly in front of the word
-word	To NOT a term, use a minus sign directly in front of the word

or you can use the full range of Boolean operators, plus nesting:

AND

OR

NOT (you can also use AND NOT)

( )

Example:

(bison OR buffalo) AND brucellosis AND transmission

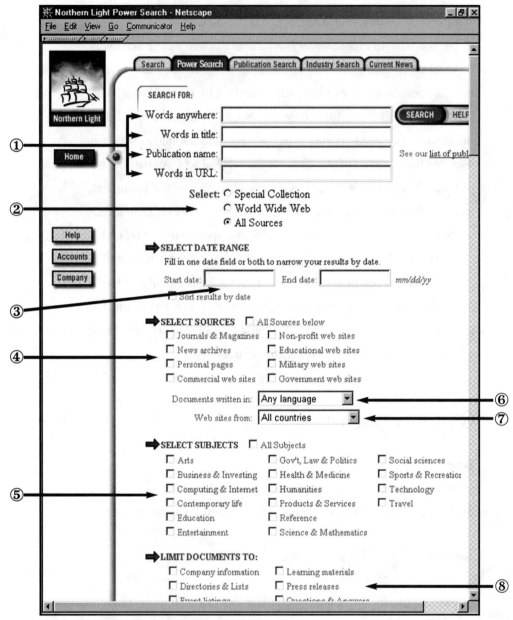

Figure 7.2   Northern Light Power Search page

Northern Light Power Search Page Options
① **Query boxes,** allowing searching in all fields, in title field, publication
   name, or by URL
② **Choice of Searching:**
     • All Sources—World Wide Web and Special Collection
     • World Wide Web   • Special Collection

③ **Select Date Range**—Can select beginning date or end date for searches, and allows sorting of results by date

④ **Select Sources:**
- All Sources
- Journals & Magazines
- News archives
- Personal pages
- Commercial Web sites

- Non-profit Web sites
- Military Web sites
- Educational Web sites
- Government Web sites

Under Select Sources, you can also specify:

⑤ **Select Subjects:**
- Arts
- Computing & Internet
- Education
- Travel
- Humanities
- Reference
- Science & Mathematics
- Sports & Recreation
- Government, Law & Politics

- Business & Investing
- Contemporary Life
- Entertainment
- Health & Medicine
- Products & Services
- Regional
- Social Sciences
- Technology

⑥ **Language**
- All languages
- French
- Italian

- English
- German
- Spanish

⑦ **Web sites from (country):** All or any one of 19 countries

⑧ **Limit Documents To:**
- Company information
- Event listings
- Job listings
- Press releases
- Reviews

- Directories & Lists
- For Sale
- Learning materials
- Questions & Answers

Truncation

Northern Light provides extensive truncation (wild card) capability:

*   for right hand truncation

Example:

comput*

%   use a percent sign for embedded truncation

Example: workm%n

This works for any single character. The % can be used more than once in a term, and the * and % can be used in the same term. A minimum of five initial characters is required (i.e., you can search for techn*, but tech* will not work).

When Northern Light ranks by relevance, it will not take into consideration those words that were retrieved by use of the wild cards. If the stem you used is a word in itself, that word will be ranked. For example, if you searched for computer*, the word "computer" will factor into the ranking, whereas those with the word "computerization" will not.

Phrase/Proximity Searching

Use double quotation marks to search for phrases. No other proximity options are available.

Searching by document type is made possible by artificial intelligence programs that recognize document types (such as recipes, interviews, etc.) by the general form and other characteristics of the particular type of document.

Name Searching

Northern Light is case-insensitive and cannot distinguish between "Frank" and "frank." To search for names, use double quotation marks. You may want to capitalize the name, so you can copy and paste it into other engines.

Example: "Dwight D. Eisenhower"

Field Searching

When it made its debut in August 1997, Northern Light promised that it would be making significant additions to its searching functionality. It has indeed done so, not only with the addition of full Boolean capabilities, but also with the addition of one of the best field searching capabilities of all the Web search engines. For Web documents, title and URL fields are searchable and for many documents there is an industry field that can be searched. For documents in the proprietary collection, you can search by publication name, by company, by ticker symbol, by industry, and—for a few types of documents—by document type. Date can be searched in Power Search, and results can be *sorted* by date when doing a Power Search, a Publication Search, an Industry Search, or a Current News Search.

In the home page version, the title, URL, company, ticker symbol, and publication fields are searchable by the use of prefixes. In Power Search mode, text boxes and lists are used to search specific fields.

URL

In the home page version of Northern Light, the URL prefix is used to specify that words occur in the URL.

Examples: url:whale:simmons

url:whale.simmons.edu

url:simmons.edu/archives

In Power Search mode, to search URL, enter the terms in the "Words in URL" box.

Title

On Northern Light's home page, Publication Search, Industry Search, and Current News page, use the title prefix to specify title words.

Example: title:field searching

title:"online strategies"

In Power Search, Industry Search, and Current News, enter the terms in the "Words in title" box. In Publication Search, use the "Words anywhere" box.

Date

Date is searchable only on the Power Search page and the Industry Search page. A start date and/or an end date can be entered in the Select Date Range boxes using the format, mm/dd/yy.

Example: 06/11/96

On the Power Search page, results can also be sorted by date (Click the "Sort results by date" box under "Select Date Range.")

On the Publication Search page, date is not searchable but results can be sorted by date.

In Current News searches, you can specify "Last Two Hours," "Today's News," or "Last Two Weeks." Results can be sorted by date and time.

Publication (Applies Only to the Special Collection)

Publication titles (such as American Mathematical Monthly) can be searched on the Power Search page (see Figure 7.2 on page 134) using the pub: prefix.

Example: pub: "Agricultural History"

Publication titles can also be searched on the Publications Page by entering the title in the "Publications name" box (see Figure 7.5 on page 143).

Company (Applies Only to the Special Collection)

To search for a company, use the company prefix on Northern Light's home page or in Power Search mode.

Example: company:"General Motors"

Ticker (Applies Only to the Special Collection)

To search for a company using the ticker symbol, use the ticker prefix on Northern Light's home page or in Power Search mode.

Example: ticker:bur

Text

Use of the text prefix is necessary when entering a Boolean expression that is a combination text and field search. If the prefix is not used, the "text" word will only be searched in the field you just specified.

Examples: text:apparel

URL:onstrat AND text:faculty

Industry

The Industry "field" is searchable using checkboxes on the "Industry Search" page. One or more selected industries or "All Industries" can be selected.

Document Type

In Power Search mode, results can be limited to any of the following document types:

- Company information
- Event listings
- Directories & Lists
- For Sale

- Job listings
- Press releases
- Reviews
- Learning materials
- Questions & Answers

According to Northern Light representatives, additional categories will be added.

When doing an Industry Search, a choice of three document types (press releases, product reviews, and job listings) can be specified using checkboxes.

Multiple fields can be searched at one time.

Example:

url:ibm AND title:cryptolope AND text:commerce

When searching for a phrase using the prefixes, use double quotation marks around the phrase. If you don't, the words you enter will be ANDed.

Example: pub: "Health Management"

OUTPUT

The number of results is shown at the top of the results page and up to 25 records per page are displayed.

Northern Light offers only one output format:

1. The Project Gutenberg Etext of The Cash Boy by Horatio Alger Jr.
   99% - Articles & General info: The Project Gutenberg Etext of The Cash Boy by Horatio Alger Jr. Please take a look at the important information in this header. We encourage... 06/10/96   **WWW**
   Singapore site: http://www.mirrors.org.sg/pg/etext95/cashb10.txt

The "**WWW**" at the right of the record indicates that this a Web document. Proprietary (pay-per-view) documents are indicated by the words, "SPECIAL COLLECTION."

SPECIAL OPTIONS

Custom Search Folders

Custom Search Folders are Northern Light's unique way of organizing results. When records are retrieved, they are listed by relevance on the right side of the page, but they are also organized into a selection of topic folders. These folders are created "on the fly" and records are grouped according to the unique characteristics of the particular search. Northern Light identifies "topics" common to various of the retrieved records and creates folders for those topics. In creating these folders, over 30 document types and 15,000 subject classifications are used.

In addition to subject folders, folders may also be created for:

- Type of document (such as press releases, maps, recipes, etc.)
- Source (by domain type or source types such as personal pages, magazines, encyclopedias, etc.)
- Language

An added benefit of the folders is that they enable you to narrow the results of your current search to some degree. When you click on one of the folders that was created, the contents of that folder are divided into a new set of folders. You cannot search within a particular folder,

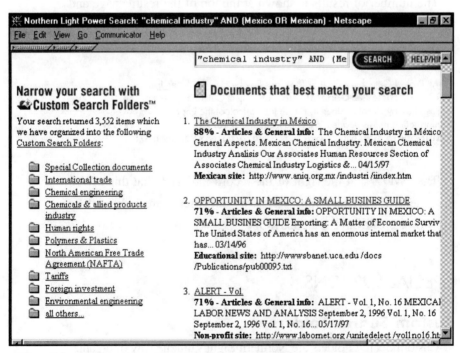

***Figure 7.3   The Northern Light results page for a search on the Mexican
chemical industry. (Notice the "folders" on the left.)***

but you can have the system narrow the results by creating the new set of categories.

For the "chemical industry in Mexico" search, the folders created are shown in Figure 7.3.

Proprietary Content (Special Collection)

In addition to searching the Web, a Northern Light search also covers over 5,000 "premium" sources including magazines, journals, newsletters, newswires, books, newspapers, and pamphlets. In results pages, these are identified by the "Special Collection" notation to the right of the item. Abstracts are shown for free and the full document can be purchased by means of a credit card. Northern Light also offers an Enterprise Account Service, which provides multiple subaccounts, direct billing, usage reports and other features.

Example:

4. <u>Hysterectomy: indications, alternatives and predictors.</u>
95% - Articles & General info: Hysterectomy, the most common major nonobstetric operation, is performed in more than 570,000 women in the United States each year.... 02/15/97
American Family Physician (magazine): Available at Northern Light

SPECIAL COLLECTION

To see a list of the titles in the Special Collection, click the Special Collection link on the home page.

Industry Search

Northern Light has assigned an industry classification to a significant number of Web pages as well as to proprietary documents. These are searched using the Industry Search page (To get to this, click on the **Industry Search** tab on Northern Light's home page.)

You can choose "**all industries**" or one or more categories. At least one of the boxes must be checked.

Twenty-six industries are identified, including:

- Accounting & Taxation
- Advertising, Marketing, Sales
- Automotive
- Health Care
- Human Resources
- Insurance

- Banking & Finance
- Biotechnology
- Chemicals & Plastics
- Computing & Internet
- Economics
- Energy & Petroleum
- Entertainment
- Environmental
- Food & Beverage
- Forest Products

- International Business
- Legal
- Management
- Manufacturing & Engineering
- Media
- Music Industry
- Pharmaceutical & Cosmetics
- Retail
- Telecommunications
- Transportation

As well as searching by subject and industry, when using the Industry Search page searches can be limited by date and by some document types (press releases, product reviews, and job listings). Within the query box, the title and the URL can be searched and, for Special Collection documents, the publication name, company

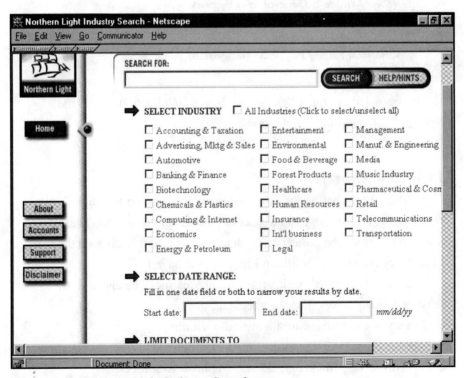

Figure 7.4   Northern Light Industry Search page

name, and ticker symbol can also be specified (see the "Field Searching" section on page 136).

Publication Search

Northern Light's Publication Search page allows you to search within a specific publication from the **Special Collection**. (To get to this, click on the **Publication Search** tab on Northern Light's home page.)

Within the query box, the title, company, and ticker symbol can also be specified, using the **title:**, **company:**, and **ticker:** prefixes respectively.

Current News

Clicking the Current News tab at the top of a Northern Light page takes you to the page that allows free access to the last two weeks of news from over seventy newswires, newsletters, and other news publications (including AP Online, UPI, PR Newswire, and others).

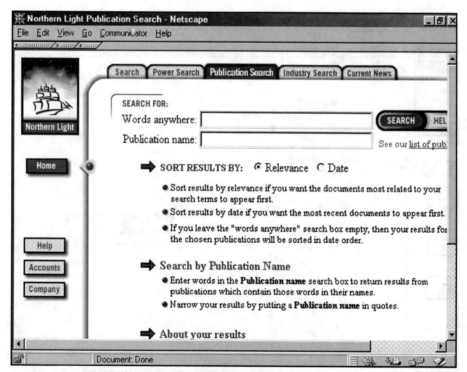

Figure 7.5   Northern Light Publication Search page

Older news from these sources is available under the other Northern Light tabs on a per-per-view basis.

Search features such as Boolean, which are available in other sections of Northern Light, are also usable here. Northern Light's news is updated every two minutes, and you can limit your search to the "last two hours," "today's news," or the last two weeks (the default). Queries can also be limited by selecting from a list of eleven news categories. Results are sorted by relevance, or they can be sorted by date and time.

Elsewhere on the Current News page are links for top headlines, weather, and sports scores, plus "Special Edition," which leads to a compilation of news and other links relating to ongoing major stories.

ADD-ONS:

Other than features such as weather and sports scores, plus "Special Edition," which leads to a compilation of news and other

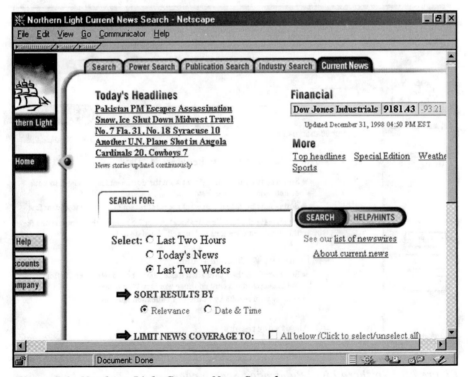

Figure 7.6 Northern Light Current News Search page

links relating to ongoing major stories found on the Current News page, Northern Light is strictly a search engine, with no add-ons.

DIRECTORY

Northern Light does not provide a directory. However, the ability to select specific subject categories on the Power Search page and the grouping of results in "folders" provides some of the classification benefits of a directory by categorizing the results of a search. Keep in mind, though, that what is included in the folders is only the results of a specific search—not a classification of the entire Northern Light database.

SUMMARY OF NORTHERN LIGHT

Northern Light, which appeared in late 1997, has a large database of Web sites and provides two significant unique features: (1) integrated searching of proprietary content, and (2) organization of results into folders. The proprietary content includes more than 5,000 magazines, journal, newswires, and other publications that can be searched either along with the Web or separately. Documents from the proprietary Special Collection can be purchased online. Northern Light's folders are very useful for identifying the context of retrieved information.

With its large and growing database, its impressive array of search options, and its performance against other engines, Northern Light is going to become the first choice for many serious searchers. For any exhaustive searches, you will want to put Northern Light on your list of engines to use. For terms that cross several fields—and when you'd like that aspect sorted out for you—be sure to use Northern Light. With the availability of a growing collection of non-Web material, this engine can provide a partial alternative to some of the higher-priced commercial search and document delivery services. If you have not tried Northern Light, do it now.

CHAPTER 8

WebCrawler
www.webcrawler.com

OVERVIEW

WebCrawler was among the first of the Web search engines and is still used by many casual searchers. It has a very simple, straightforward interface that looks very much like Excite's, which is not surprising since WebCrawler is now owned by Excite. It has a full complement of Boolean operators. Its major weakness is its low retrieval: WebCrawler often retrieves less than 5 percent of the number of records retrieved by the most comprehensive engines.

The WebCrawler database contains approximately 2 million Web pages.

Strengths 👍	Weaknesses 👎
• Familiar to many users • "Shortcuts" (related sites shown on results pages)	• Numbers of items retrieved are very low • No truncation

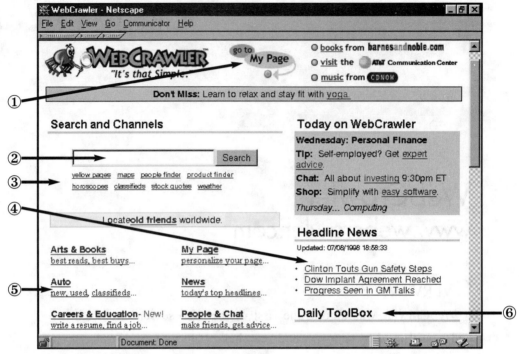

Figure 8.1   The WebCrawler home page

WebCrawler Home Page Features

Main Options Displayed on Webcrawler's Home Page

① **Link to** personalized news page

② **Query box,** where words, phrases, Boolean expressions can be entered.

③ **Links to:**

- music search
- maps
- horoscopes
- weather
- yellow pages
- product finder
- classified ads
- chat
- people finder
- books
- stock quotes

④ **Headlines**

⑤ **Directory** (Channels)

⑥ Daily featured sites

WHAT HAPPENS BEHIND THE SCENES

WebCrawler claims to support "natural language searching," using that expression fairly loosely. It does not do well with natural language entries such as "To be or not to be." Unless quotation marks are used, in this and other phrases, it interprets the words "or" and "and" as Boolean operators. Furthermore, WebCrawler ignores common words.

When multiple words are entered without any Boolean operators, WebCrawler will find all records containing any of the words. It will first present records containing all of the words, followed by the remaining records containing any of the words.

SEARCH FEATURES
Boolean Logic
AND
OR
NOT
( )

> *Examples*: (Somme OR Verdun) AND casualties
> "daily requirements" AND (vitamins OR minerals)

Alternatively, you can use:

+word   for AND, put a plus sign in front of the term
-word   for NOT, put a minus sign in front of the term

> *Example*:+pollution +rivers -Chesapeake

Truncation
Truncation is not an option, and WebCrawler does not truncate automatically.

Phrases
" "   For phrase searching, use double quotation marks.

Name Searching
No special "name searching" feature is available in Webcrawler. Use phrase searching (" ") to search for names.

Field Searching
WebCrawler has no facility for searching specific fields.

OUTPUT

WebCrawler reports the results of a search as:

(25 of 1250)

The searcher has the option of either a summary format (the default) or a title format. By means of the link just above the results, you can change to the other format option. The percent figure shown in the summary format is the relevance score.

Title Format

- Woodmaster Foundations Inc.
- ContractorNet - Original Source for Credible Contractors
- Tips for the Home Buyer: RADON
- The Livable Basement

Summary Format (default)

75% Dust Mite News

Individuals who sweat a lot, go to bed with wet hair or sleep under piles of blankets most likely have higher bedding moisture and therefore higher levels of mite colonization.) In one home I actually found that despite high levels of mite allergens in all carpeting, the air in the asthmatic sons room with a HEPA cleaner operating was the most irritating. Similar Pages
http://kalypso.cybercom.net/~jmhi/mite.html

SPECIAL OPTIONS

"Shortcuts"

On results pages, WebCrawler may show a selection of Shortcuts. These are links to sites related to the query that come from the WebCrawler Guide, plus links to the Barnes & Noble and CDNOW sites, maps, stock quotes, and weather forecasts. In Figure 8.2 you can see these links on the right side of the page.

When your search includes a U.S. city, links to a map and the weather forecast for that city automatically appear in the Shortcuts column.

ADD-ONS

Webcrawler add-ons include:

- WebCrawler Guide (WebCrawler's directory, the same as Excite)

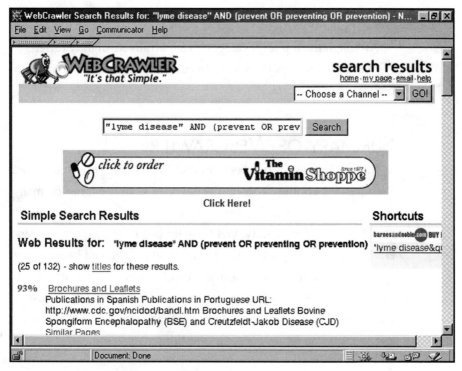

Figure 8.2   A WebCrawler results page

- Personalized news page (personalized news, events, weather, etc.)
- Music search (the CDNOW online music and video store)
- Yellow pages (from Zip2)
- People finder (phone number and email address lookup from AnyWho)
- Maps
- Horoscopes
- Classifieds (search or place free classified ads through the Classifieds 2000 Network)
- Stock quotes (stock and mutual fund prices, personal portfolio, etc.)
- Weather (local weather and weather links)
- Headlines (from Reuters)
- Product Finder (online shopping)
- Books (Barnes & Noble)
- Chat (Chat rooms and message boards)

WEBCRAWLER'S DIRECTORY

Although the top level categories are arranged slightly differently, WebCrawler uses the same directory as Excite (its parent). For details, see Chapter 3.

SUMMARY OF WEBCRAWLER

Mainly because it has been around for a (relatively) long time, WebCrawler continues to be the favorite search engine of many casual searchers. The operative phrase for the serious searcher is "has been." Unfortunately, WebCrawler just hasn't kept up. It generally retrieves only a tiny portion of what is retrieved by the other major engines. If you are a serious searcher who works with, or for, casual Web searchers (some of whom may be loyal Webcrawler users), you might want to get to know WebCrawler simply to make it easier for you to answer their questions.

Yahoo!
www.yahoo.com

OVERVIEW

Yahoo!, one of the first "finding tools" on the Web, still remains one of the strongest. This is mainly because it integrates its primary nature as a directory with indexing and a reasonable collection of search features including truncation, Boolean (minimal), and phrase searching. The producers clearly state that Yahoo! is a directory rather than a search engine; however, given its searchability and the sophisticated ways it integrates the searching and directory functions, it deserves mention in both categories.

Yahoo! indexes more than a half million Web pages. Remember that Yahoo! is primarily a directory, rather than a general search

Strengths	Weaknesses
• Extensive classified collection closely integrated into searching • Truncation • Automatic link to AltaVista • Retrieving words are highlighted	• Minimal Boolean • The Yahoo! database itself is very small

153

engine and that every page in Yahoo! reflects a selection and classification process, unlike records in search engines. It is the largest of all the Web directories.

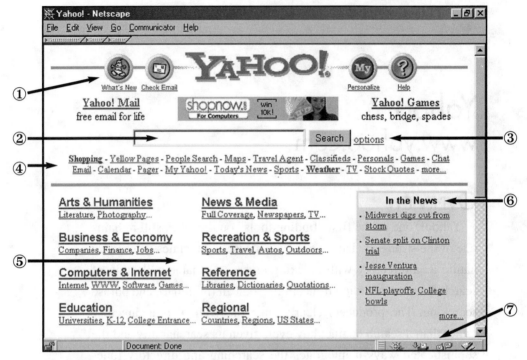

Figure 9.1   The Yahoo! home page

Yahoo! Home Page Options

① "What's New," free email, personalized page, and help links.

② **Search box** (can enter words, Boolean query, or phrases)

③ **Options** The almost-hidden "Options" link leads to the Search Options page where a variety of options are displayed

④ Add-ons:

• Shopping	• Yellow Pages	• Maps	• Message Boards	• Email
• Stock Quotes	• Personals	• Classifieds	• Today's News	• Sports
• Weather	• Chat	• TV	• White Pages	• etc.

   • My Yahoo! (personalized page)   • Pager (for emailing people currently online)

⑤ The top level Yahoo! classification

⑥ Headlines

⑦ On lower portion of page (not shown here):

• Featured sites	• Country-specific versions of Yahoo!
• Metro versions of Yahoo!	• Other specialized guides (Yahooligans for kids, etc.)

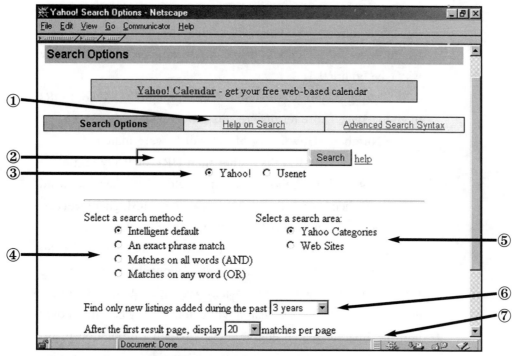

Figure 9.2 The Yahoo! "Options" page

① Help links
② Search box (can enter words, Boolean query, or phrases)
③ Choice of Yahoo! or Usenet
④ Choice of relevance ranking, phrase, AND, OR, or name
⑤ Choice of Yahoo! categories or Web Sites
⑥ Choice of date range (1 day to 3 years)
⑦ Choice of display of 10, 20, 50, or 100 results per page

WHAT HAPPENS BEHIND THE SCENES

According to its producers, Yahoo! searches through four areas of its database when a query is submitted:

- Yahoo! Categories
- Yahoo! Web Sites
- Web pages (from the Inktomi database)
- Yahoo! Net Events (such as chat sessions with personalities) and Chat
- Most recent News Articles

Categories and Web Sites will be displayed automatically. To get to news and net events, you need to click the appropriate link on a results page. Amazon books also can now be searched in the same way (see Figure 9.3).

If a string of terms is entered with no qualifiers, Yahoo! ORs them together. Those results are sorted by relevancy based on:

- Number—How many of the words were matched
- Field—Title weighs higher than URL or Body text
- Level of the Yahoo! category matched—When the word searched is a word in a Yahoo! category, the higher level category matches rank higher than deeper level categories

The first page of results displayed will be a list of Yahoo! category headings that match your search, followed by specific sites from the Yahoo! database that match (see Figure 9.3). If there are no matches for either, the search will automatically be carried over into the Inktomi search engine. (The Inktomi Corporation maintains a very large Web database that it provides to search engine services, but not directly to the public.)

By clicking on any of the search engine links at the bottom of a Yahoo! results page, your search is automatically carried into that engine (keep in mind that, as you change search engines, you may need to modify your search for compatibility of syntax).

SEARCH FEATURES

Boolean Logic

+word   To **AND** a term, use a plus sign directly in front of the word

-word   To **NOT** a term, use a minus sign directly in front of the word

Phrase Searching

" "   Use double quotation marks to search on a phrase
Example: "World War II"

Figure 9.3 A Yahoo! results page

① By clicking on the links labeled "Categories, Web Sites, Web Pages, News Stories, Net Events," you can access a list of matching News Articles, Net Events, etc.

② Matching categories are shown first (i.e., if the query words occur in any category names, those categories will be shown)

③ Clicking on a specific level within the category heading will take you to that level

④ After category matches, site matches are shown

Truncation

*   Use an asterisk to truncate a search phrase

   Example: manufact*

Although it is not documented, Yahoo! apparently performs automatic truncation. For example, the query virgin airlines yielded the following:

   Regional: U.S. States: **Virgin**ia: Cities: Woodbridge: Business and Shopping: Companies: Transportation

   • Aviation Analysts, Inc. - assists air traffic service providers, civil aviation authorities, airlines and airports in implementing air traffic control solutions.

***Figure 9.4** This is the Yahoo! page that results from clicking on the cryptography classification. Notice the link to three Usenet groups indicated by the Usenet link followed by the number "3."*

Conveniently, Yahoo! highlights the search terms responsible for retrieving a given record. 👍

Name Searching

Yahoo! is case-insensitive and cannot distinguish between "White" and "white." To get the effect of name searching, search using double quotes. You may want to capitalize the name, so you can copy and paste it most effectively into other engines.

Example: "King Arthur"

Field Searching

t: for title

Example: t:Bell Atlantic

u: for URL

        Example: u:intel

Order of Syntax

If you mix the Boolean and the field search features in the same statement, the operators must be applied in this order: + - t: u:

OUTPUT

Yahoo! provides one standard output format. Records are listed in relevance-ranked order.

On the options page there is a choice of 10, 20, 50 or 100 records to be displayed per page.

Standard Output:

Entertainment: Food and Eating: Recipes
Cuccina Brucce's Favorite Foods - ribs, frijoles, fondue, crowue monsieiur, salsa, hummus and other family favorites.

SPECIAL OPTIONS

Personalization

Yahoo! has a personalized page ("My Yahoo!) to rival that provided by Excite. To get to the personal page, look for the small "Personalize" (under the "MY" button) link at the top of Yahoo!'s home page. With My Yahoo! you can specify which categories of news you would like to see, set up a detailed personal portfolio, view the weather, and further make the page fit your own interests. Perhaps most importantly, with Yahoo!'s News Clipper service you can set up your own current awareness searches.

Transfer of Your Search to Other Engines

A unique feature of Yahoo! is the automatic transfer of a search into a variety of other engines. This makes Yahoo! a good starting place for searches in which it will be useful to look at a limited number of select pages first before searching more broadly. Look at the bottom of results pages for links to other search engines. By clicking on these, the query will be transferred automatically without your having to retype it. Once at the other search engine's site, however, you should check the syntax to make sure it is compatible.

Country, Regional, and City-Specific Versions

At the bottom of Yahoo!'s home page are links to specialized versions of Yahoo! for 16 countries and regions, plus local Yahoo!s for 12 U.S. cities.

ADD-ONS

- Yellow Pages—As well as finding addresses and phone numbers, if you enter a location, Yahoo! identifies businesses closest to you.
- White Pages—Search for addresses, phone numbers, email addresses, and home pages.
- Maps—Look at maps for U.S. addresses (using MapQuest)
- Classifieds—Search online classifieds by location, topic, etc.
- Personals—Search personal classifieds (the ones with all the interesting abbreviations)
- Chat—View the usual thoughtful, sophisticated repartee
- Email—Use a free email account
- Message Boards—Post and read messages
- My Yahoo!—Personalize your page
- Pager—Send instant messages to and from others currently online
- Sports—Obtain Sports Scores
- Today's News—View Yahoo!'s News headlines, summaries
- TV—See TV listings
- Weather—Check out the weather
- Stock Quotes—The market, business news, stock quotes, portfolio, etc.
- Shopping—Unlimited opportunities to spend money online

Yahoo!'s Classification

The classification of sites is Yahoo!'s greatest and most unique strength. No other search engine has the depth of classification provided by Yahoo!, and only Yahoo! incorporates the assigned classifications so directly into its search algorithm. At various levels in the classification hierarchy, you can choose to search just within that category.

Yahoo! typically provides from four to six levels of classification. The top level classes are:

- Arts and Humanities
- Computers and Internet
- Entertainment
- Health
- Recreation and Sports
- Regional
- Social Science

- Business and Economy
- Education
- Government
- News and Media
- Reference
- Science
- Society and Culture

Examples of levels and sublevels are:

Regional
  Countries
    Russia
      Business and Economy
        Companies
          Trade
            Organizations
Social Science
  Political Science
    International Relations
      Conferences

The output shown in Figure 9.5 (see page 162) is the result of clicking down through the hierarchy to a fourth level. You will see that there is still at least one additional level and that there are also sites specifically classified at this level.

The classification is not totally linear, as there are cross-classifications. For example, you will find Psychology under Health, and also under Science. When you follow the Health class down to Psychology, you will suddenly notice that you are no longer in the Health category, but in Science.

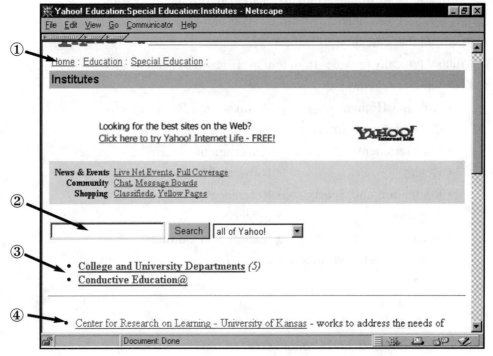

Figure 9.5 Yahoo! listings under "Education-Special Education-Institutes"

① Review of the position in the hierarchy
② Option to enter a query and search either all of Yahoo! or only within the current class. Note that you can search within the category at any level.
③ Additional levels still available
④ Sites classified at this level

SUMMARY OF YAHOO!

Yahoo!, as its producers clearly state, is not really a general search engine. It is included in this book because—although it is indeed a directory—it exhibits many of the characteristics of a search engine and integrates those searching functions extremely well into the directory functions. As the best known, largest, and arguably the best general purpose Web directory, it should be considered whenever browsing rather than searching is the aim. It can help you avoid having to look at a large number of sites when only a small set of search answers is desirable. Since pages must meet Yahoo!'s editorial criteria to be entered into the database, the average quality of retrieved sites tends to be higher than with other search services.

The serious searcher will also want to take a look at "My Yahoo!," with its News Clipper service providing personalized current awareness searches.

CHAPTER 10

Meta-Search Engines

"ALL-IN-ONE" SEARCH PAGES

With eight or more major search engines available, wouldn't it be wonderful to have a means to search a number of them at once? Great idea! The good news is that it is possible and there are dozens of sites that allow you to search multiple engines simultaneously. The bad news is that the results often fall short of what you might expect.

These services are usually referred to as "meta-search sites," or "all-in-one" search sites. Though these services have their advantages, there are drawbacks. In particular, if there are more than a handful of relevant sites to be found in the Web search engines, the meta-search engines often miss most of them. This is caused by a number of factors, including limits imposed by the service on the number of records retrieved from individual engines, time-outs where the meta-search service simply cuts off the search within an engine if it takes too long, failure to adequately translate the query into the specific syntax required by the target engine, and other factors. Fortunately, at least two meta-search engines—Dogpile and Internet Sleuth—appear to be addressing this problem, and more are likely to follow their lead.

Creating one of these sites is not difficult, which helps account for their large number. Yahoo!'s category for these engines lists over

130 of them. Some are basically a collection of search boxes that have been copied and pasted from the various search engines. Most search engine producers are more than happy to have their mini-interfaces copied onto as many sites as possible, since it generates traffic to their own sites.

For the most part, the meta-search engines differ from one another in the following ways:

- The specific search engines they cover
- The number of search engines that can be searched at a time
- Their ability to transfer more sophisticated queries—such as those including phrases, Boolean statements, etc.—to the "target" search engines
- Their limits on how many records they can retrieve from each engine (which can be as low as ten)
- The length of time they are willing to spend searching each engine (time-out)
- How output is presented
- Whether or not they eliminate duplicate hits from the various engines

The three major weaknesses of meta-search engines are (1) they often strictly limit the number of records they will retrieve from any single engine (sometimes to as few as ten); (2) they often will not transfer even slightly sophisticated queries to the engines; and (3) in most cases they do not search some of the largest search engines—often neglecting HotBot and Northern Light.

Many of these meta-search sites can be used effectively if for your particular search you think that there exist fewer than ten sites of interest (or you don't care to identify more than ten sites) and your search only involves a single word or phrase.

The meta-search engines are most useful when you are looking for something very obscure. There are many records that are found in some of the smaller engines that are not retrieved by any of the three or four largest engines and it can be time-consuming to individually search all of the major engines. The meta-search engines do indeed allow you to very quickly scan many engines for that obscure term or phrase.

It is not feasible to cover all 130-plus of these meta-search engines here. Instead, we will look at six of the more popular ones. These six aptly demonstrate the variety of approaches taken:

- Dogpile—www.dogpile.com
- Inference Find—www.infind.com
- Internet Sleuth—www.isleuth.com
- MetaCrawler—www.metacrawler.com
- ProFusion—www.profusion.com.
- SavvySearch—www.savvysearch.com

For an extensive list of meta-search sites, in Yahoo! go to:

Computers and Internet:Internet: World Wide Web:Searching the Web: All-in-One Search Pages

(www.yahoo.com/Computers_and_ Internet/Internet/World_Wide_Web/ Searching_the_Web/All_in_One_ Search_Pages/)

DOGPILE
www.dogpile.com

Dogpile is a meta-search engine that seems to identify and retrieve basically the same records from the target engines as are retrieved when those engines are searched individually. Dogpile translates queries into the nearest similar syntax for each of the target engines. This allows Boolean and proximity queries to work quite well.

Dogpile allows a choice of searching the Web, Usenet, FTP, or newswires.

Figure 10.1 The Dogpile home page

By clicking Custom Search, you can specify the order in which queries are sent to the various engines. Engines may also be deleted from the list of those to be searched.

Dogpile provides a link to another meta-search engine, Metafind, which searches fewer engines, using a different syntax and output order.

Dogpile Searches These Services:
World Wide Web:

- Yahoo!
- Lycos' A2Z
- Go2.com
- What U Seek
- Lycos
- PlanetSearch
- Magellan
- WebCrawler
- Infoseek
- AltaVista
- Excite
- Thunderstone
- Excite Guide

Usenet:

- Reference.com
- AltaVista
- Deja News
- Deja News' archival database

FTP:

- Filez and FTP Search

Newswires:

- Excite News
- Others
- Yahoo! News Headlines
- Infoseek News Wires

Search Syntax

To the degree to which each of the engines accepts it, Dogpile transmits AND, OR, NEAR operators, parentheses, and quotation marks. In some cases it translates the query to make it appropriate to the receiving engine, such as changing NEAR to AND if the receiving engine does not support NEAR. Dogpile's documentation covers these details very well.

Waiting Time Permitted

The user can select to have Dogpile wait up to 60 seconds for responses to answers from the search engines.

Limits on Number of Records

Dogpile imposes no limits on the number of records retrieved.

Arrangement of Output

Output is arranged by search engine.

Author's Note: Thunderstone and Planet Search (search engines many searchers have never heard of) often come out in Dogpile searches as the leaders in terms of number of hits. This is due to the fact that when multiterm searches are entered in Dogpile and submitted to those engines, they treat words in the query with a default OR, regardless of the original query syntax. This can result in the retrieval of very large numbers of non-relevant records.

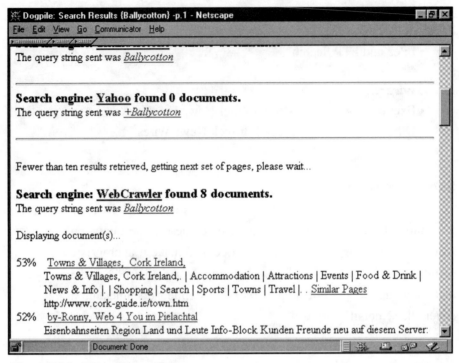

Figure 10.2 A Dogpile results page

INFERENCE FIND
www.infind.com

Inference Find searches six engines, and its major strength is the very convenient way results are presented. Retrieved pages are "clustered" by site and type of site, with duplicates eliminated. As with most other meta-search engines, Inference Find often returns far fewer records than would be found through individual searches of the search engines themselves.

Engines Searched:
- WebCrawler
- Yahoo!
- Lycos
- AltaVista
- Infoseek
- Excite

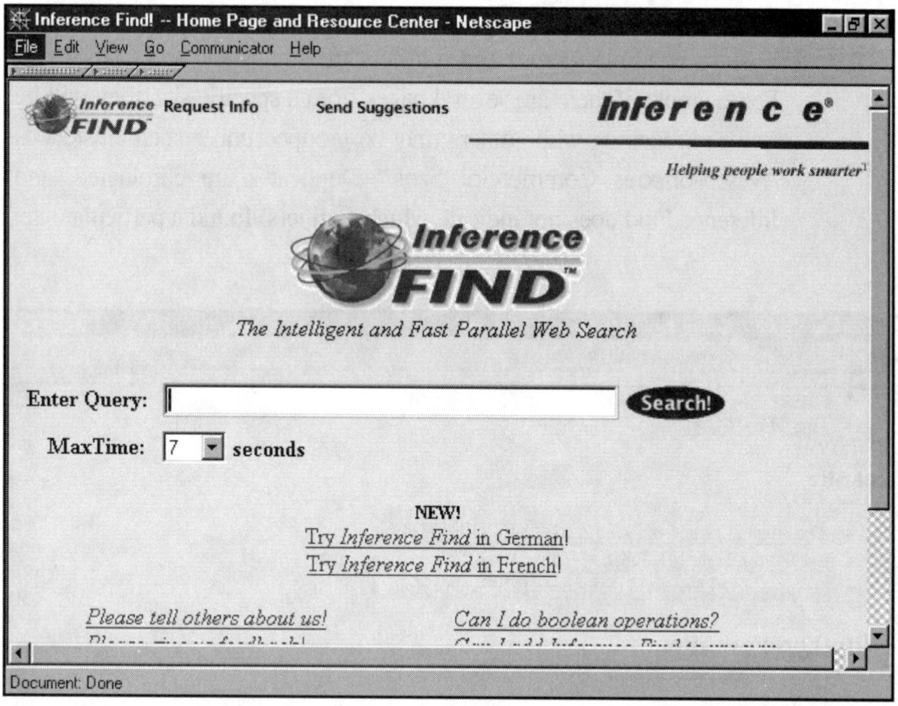

Figure 10.3 The Inference Find home page

Search Syntax

Queries are transmitted to the target engines just as entered by the user. Therefore, if the searcher enters a Boolean query and a target engine cannot handle it, results will not necessarily be what was requested.

Waiting Time Permitted

On the home page, the user can specify a maximum waiting time of 1, 5, 7, 10 or 30 seconds per engine. On results pages, there is a query box and 60 seconds is also allowed.

Limits on Number of Records

There seems to be no specific limit to the number of records retrieved with Inference Find, other than that determined by the specified time-out. In effect, the total maximum number retrieved is in the vicinity of 200.

Arrangement of Output

Inference Find merges and "clusters" results by site and type of site. For example, if there are several pages from a specific site, they will be grouped together, while others may be grouped under such clusters as "Miscellaneous Commercial Sites." Duplicates are eliminated, and Inference Find does not indicate which engine(s) found a particular site.

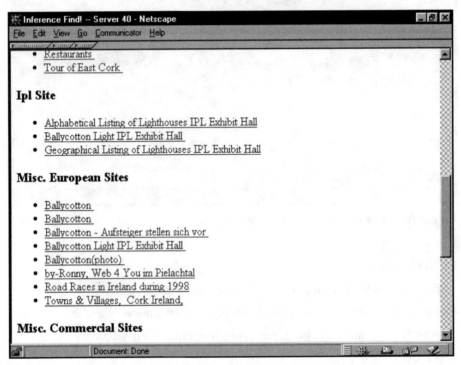

Figure 10.4 An example of a page of output from Inference Find, showing arrangement of sites by clusters

INTERNET SLEUTH
www.isleuth.com

In addition to providing a meta-search of six search engines, Internet Sleuth also provides a searchable directory of over 3,000 databases on the Web, arranged in about 300 categories. These include very large databases such as MEDLINE and ERIC, small ones such as the contents of individual journals, plus indexes to directories such

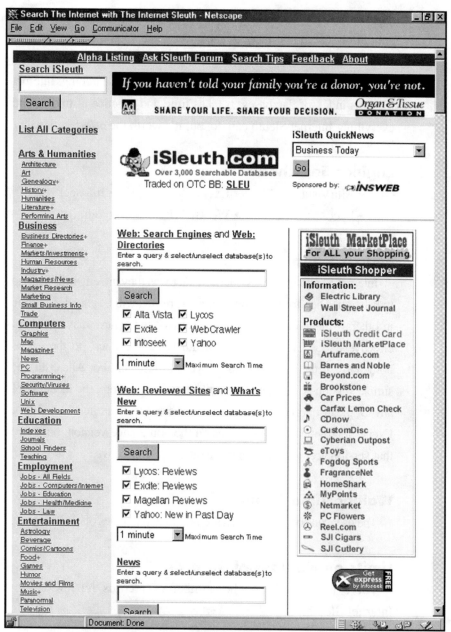

Figure 10.5 The Internet Sleuth home page

as WWW Virtual Library and Infomine. (Internet Sleuth does not search those databases, it searches the directory listing for the databases to enable identification of databases relevant to a particular subject area.) It does, however, provide a somewhat customized, often very simplified search interface for each individual database.

There are two search boxes on the Internet Sleuth home page: one for searching the search engines, the other for searching Internet Sleuth's index of databases. It takes time and practice to understand everything Internet Sleuth can do, but it's worth the effort.

Engines Searched

- AltaVista
- Excite
- Infoseek
- Lycos
- WebCrawler
- Yahoo

Search Syntax

Internet Sleuth transmits queries exactly as they are entered, with no translation. Therefore, for some engines, results will be excellent, while in others—including AltaVista and Lycos—the syntax may not work effectively. For Lycos, Internet Sleuth sends the query to the Lycos home page version rather than to Lycos Pro Search. For AltaVista, the simple version is searched. For both engines, therefore, the meaning of any Boolean queries submitted by Internet Sleuth is invalidated. For Excite, Internet Sleuth also relies on the home page version, but since that version accepts Boolean those queries are effective.

Waiting Time Permitted

The user can specify from ten seconds to two minutes of waiting time.

Limits on Number of Records

There is no limit on the number of records retrieved with Internet Sleuth.

Arrangement of Output

Internet Sleuth's output is *arranged by search engine*. The main features, options, etc., found in the "native" version of the target search engines are shown and can be accessed directly from Internet Sleuth's results pages.

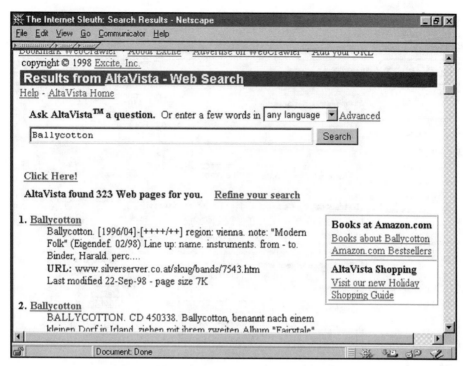

Figure 10.6 An Internet Sleuth results page

METACRAWLER

www.metacrawler.com

MetaCrawler, now a part of Go2Net, Inc., was one of the first meta-search sites. Two versions, Home Page and Power Search, are available. The latter provides additional functionality with domain searching (continent, .edu, .com, .gov, etc.), and the ability to specify timeout, number of results per page, and number of results per source (10, 20, or 30). Both versions provide limited Boolean capabilities by allowing the choice of "any" or "all" words, or phrase searching.

Engines/Directories Searched

- AltaVista
- Excite
- Infoseek
- Lycos
- WebCrawler
- Yahoo!
- Thunderstone
- The Mining Co.
- LookSmart

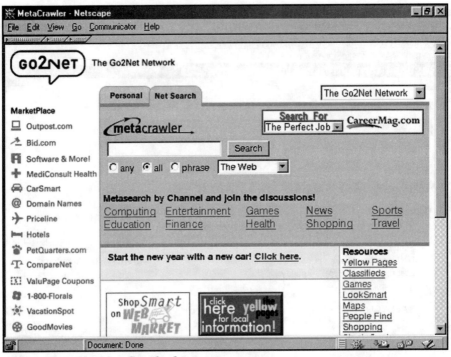

Figure 10.7 The MetaCrawler home page

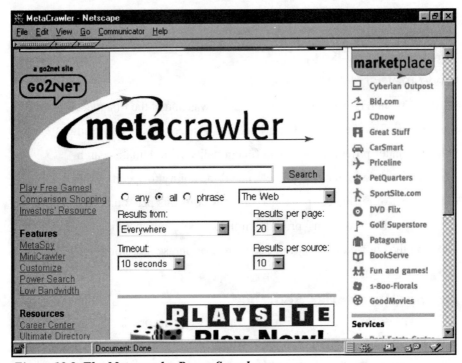

Figure 10.8 The Metacrawler Power Search page

Search Syntax

The searcher can specify that "any," "all," or "as a phrase" be applied to the words in the query. For Boolean, +word and -word can be used. This "least common denominator" query is then transmitted to the target engines

Waiting Time Permitted

In Power Search, a time-out of up to two minutes can be specified.

Limits on Number of Records

With MetaCrawler's home page version, up to ten records per engine can be retrieved. In Power Search mode, the user can specify 10, 20, or 30 records per source.

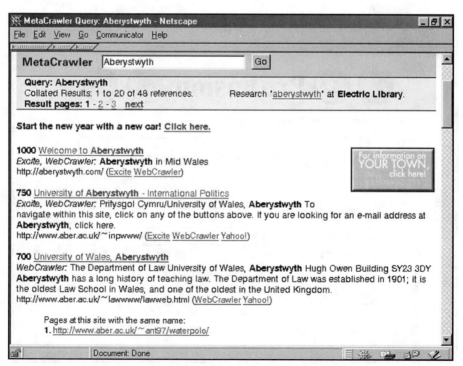

Figure 10.9 A MetaCrawler results page

Arrangement of Output

Output is *arranged by relevance ranking*. MetaCrawler determines relevance by combining and normalizing the scores given by the various engines and expressing the resultant score as a number between 1 and 1,000. In the case of duplicates, MetaCrawler will list the site only once, but it will show which engines found the site and the detail provided by each engine.

PROFUSION

www.profusion.com

ProFusion has what appears to be one of the most sophisticated and flexible structures and has tremendous promise. However, most of the sophistication is wasted because of the fact that ProFusion imposes very small maximums (10–25) on the number of records it will retrieve from each engine.

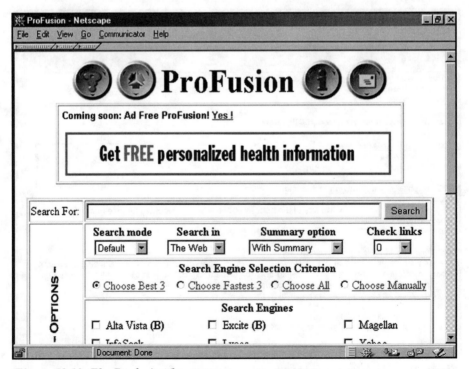

Figure 10.10 The Profusion home page

A unique feature unique among meta-search engines is ProFusion's alerting service, ProFusion Personal Assistant. This feature allows the entry of searches that ProFusion will run automatically every week, every two weeks, or once per month, with results sent via email.

ProFusion also provides the option of checking links to see if they are active.

Engines Searched:

- AltaVista
- Excite
- GoTo
- Infoseek
- Lycos
- Magellan
- Snap
- WebCrawler
- Yahoo!

Of these, you can choose to search:

- The "Best 3"
- The "Fastest 3"
- All

You can also "manually" choose engines you wish to search. If you choose manually, be sure to check the "Choose Manually" box. Just clicking the selected engines will not work.

Search Syntax

Next to the checkboxes for selecting the engines you want to search, ProFusion gives an indication (with a "B") as to whether the engine supports Boolean queries. It supports full Boolean (AND, OR, NOT) plus NEAR. For the engines that have Boolean, but not NEAR (Excite and WebCrawler), ProFusion changes NEAR to an AND.

This feature provides very useful user control over the search and knowledge as to what is taking place in the search.

If you wish to use Boolean queries, you must choose "Boolean" in the "Search mode" box.

Waiting Time Permitted

ProFusion does not provide a waiting time option, nor does it specify what time limit may be set automatically by the system.

Limits on Number of Records

ProFusion limits retrieval to either 10, 20, or 25 records, depending on the search engines selected.

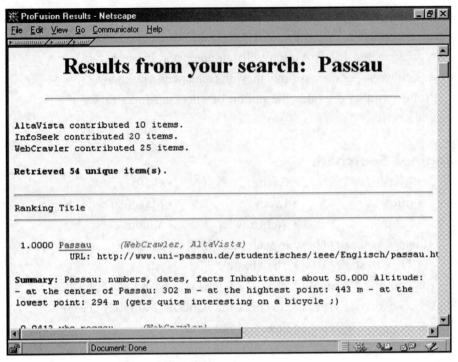

Figure 10.11 A Profusion results page

Arrangement of Output

ProFusion eliminates duplicates and lists them according to a relevance ranking score.

SavvySearch

www.savvysearch.com

SavvySearch provides a gateway to a collection of over 150 search engines, directories, online stores, Usenet archives, news archives, software libraries, etc. On its main page these are categorized under "Search," "Specialty," and "Shop." To get to search engines, click on "Search Engines" under the Search category.

The SavvySearch interface is available in 20 languages.

Figure 10.12 The SavvySearch home page

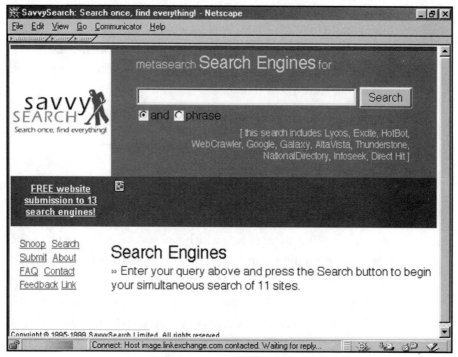

Figure 10.13 The SavvySearch "Search Engines" page

New Experimental Interface

This experimental version of SavvySearch provides more detail as to which sources are searched in each grouping.

Engines Searched

In addition to searching other tools, SavvySearch offers the option of searching the following general search engines:

• AltaVista	• Excite	• Infoseek
• Lycos	• WebCrawler	• Google
• Direct Hit	• Thunderstone	• HotBot

Search Syntax

Users can choose to have query words either ANDed or searched as a phrase by clicking on the appropriate radio button beneath the query box.

Arrangement of Output

SavvySearch presents results for five engines at a time. Click on the "search more engines" link to see the results from the next set of engines. Up to 20 records per page will be displayed. To see the next 20 records from the current set of engines, click on "next."

Next to the title of each record you will see the engine(s) in which that record was found.

OTHER META-SEARCH ENGINES— OTHER APPROACHES

We can look forward to new meta-search engines popping up fairly frequently, often using unique and creative approaches. The idea of "intelligent agents," which go several steps beyond the meta-search engines that have been discussed here, will become more and more prominent. Most noted among these at the moment is Copernic, which, by means of a program downloaded to the user's computer, searches a variety of Web search engines, sorts out the results, allows further local searching of that data, and performs a variety of related tasks. Keep an eye on these.

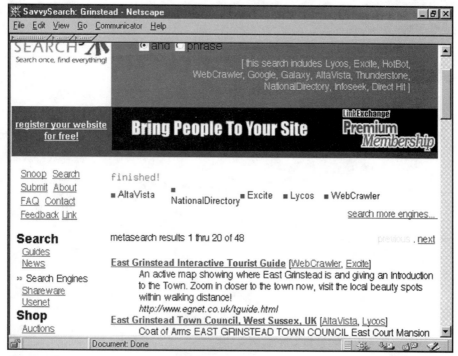

Figure 10.14 A SavvySearch results page

Infoseek Express (see page 110) is another example of such a program.

SUMMARY OF META-SEARCH ENGINES

Though there are many meta-search engines, few of them are truly effective. In using a meta-search engine, your query may not be transferred in an appropriate form to the target search engines; thus you may not get all the records you would if you searched the engines individually. Currently, at least one meta-search engine, Dogpile, appears to find all the records that would be found individually in the various engines.

Meta-search engines are most useful when you have a question that consists of a single word or phrase and you expect that word or phrase to return very few records. Try these search services, but don't get too excited about them yet.

CHAPTER 11

Other Search Engines and Further Reading

OTHER SEARCH ENGINES

The search engines that have been discussed in this book are the larger, more powerful and more popular ones. They are also services that have the intent of covering a significant portion of the Web without any limitation in terms of subject area or geographic origin (though it can be argued that Web sites from the United States are disproportionately indexed). There are many other search engines available on the Web. Indeed, in the narrower, perhaps even more legitimate sense of the term, any site that is "searchable" has a search engine. More to the point, though, is that there are a number of search engines that focus on Web sites from a particular geographic area—the U.K., for instance—or apply some other criteria that limit their coverage.

For an extensive list of search engines, try the following category in Yahoo!:

Computers and Internet:Internet:World Wide Web:Searching the Web:Search Engines

FURTHER READING

Search Engine Watch

searchenginewatch.com

Danny Sullivan of Calafia Consulting has created and maintains a site, Search Engine Watch, which provides up-to-date reports and news about all the major search engines. His slant is a little more toward providing information for Website creators than for information searchers, but he covers the user's side quite well. He provides a wide range of information—technical and not-so-technical—about search engines, and he does so in a concise, readable style. Access to portions of the site is free, but a subscription is required to access the more in-depth resources. If you are a search engine maven, be sure to visit Search Engine Watch.

Free Pint

www.freepint.co.uk

Free Pint, from William Hann, is a free fortnightly email newsletter for Web searchers. It contains helpful tips and articles on how to get quality results from Web sources.

The Mining Company Guide to Web Search

websearch.miningco.com

Chris Sherman runs this very informative site that tracks search engine news, changes, and features and also includes articles on searching, a bulletin board, and other options. In connection with the site, he publishes a free email newsletter covering search engines, Web Search Newsletter.

Journals

For current articles revelant to making the most effective use of search engines, try the following:

Searcher: The Magazine for Database Professionals
Information Today, 143 Old Marlton Pike, Medford, NJ 08055
www.infotoday.com

Online: The Leading Magazine for Information Professionals
Online, Inc., 213 Danbury Road, Wilton, CT 06897
www.onlineinc.com

Database: The Magazine of Electronic Research and Resources
Online, Inc., 213 Danbury Road, Wilton, CT 06897
www.onlineinc.com

The CyberSkeptic's Guide to Internet Research
Bibliodata, P.O. Box 61, Needham Heights, MA 02494
www.bibliodata.com

CHAPTER 12

Conclusion

Hopefully, this book has provided you with a better sense of what search engines can do for you and how you can best take advantage of what they offer. As you've seen, there is a lot of power hidden behind the populist-based interfaces. Beyond what this book may have been able to accomplish, the best way to really get to know the engines well is to use them. I don't recommend trying to know all of them in detail, or for that matter trying to remember much detail at all. I do recommend starting out with a couple of the engines, perhaps the largest ones, and become intimately acquainted with these. Click every link you can find on the home page, then do the same for the next level of pages. Read the documentation, but remain skeptical.

Do some benchmark testing of your own. Choose a topic with a limited number of likely results and run the search on two engines. Compare the individual records each retrieves. For the records that are retrieved by both engines, study the way they are ranked. Increase your own searching repertoire by trying out the unique features of each engine, and try searching fields you haven't thought to search before.

If there is one basic rule for success in using search engines, it is this: If you really want to find the best and most complete information on your topic, use more than one engine. Beyond that, if you think that even one engine is going to retrieve more material than you can use, try refining your question. If you can, make your question precise enough that only a few records are likely to be retrieved. Then perform that same search on the second engine. You'll often be surprised at the number of good (or even better) records the second engine will deliver.

As you become acquainted with the nuances of the various engines, you'll come to recognize changes made by the producers. Add-ons will continually be added. With luck, some powerful search features will be added, while other features will be discontinued. At any time, a new fad can hit, with at least half of the engines jumping on the bandwagon to provide, for instance, a recipe service, a calculator, tide tables, or whatever else the "me-too" marketers consider "hot." Forgive them, for they are still learning, and they have a long way to go.

Patience is probably the single most important personal characteristic for success in using Web search engines. Your patience will pay off. You will improve your own skills, and you will see improvements in the various search engines. These engines and the Web they search already provide us with new and sometimes rather amazing research capabilities. Stay tuned, because it's going to get even better.

GLOSSARY

SEARCH ENGINE-RELATED TERMS

Author's Note: The following terms and phrases are defined in the context of Web search engines and may not be applicable in other contexts.

add-ons. Features and services attached to a search engine that are not directly a part of the searching function.

algorithm. A step-by-step procedure for solving a problem or achieving a task. In the context of search engines, the part of the service's program that performs a task such as identifying which pages should be retrieved or the ranking of pages that have been retrieved.

alternate text. In the HTML code for Web pages, the text that goes along with an image file and is to be displayed if for some reason the image does not display. In addition to that use, it can be useful for retrieval purposes for identifying and indexing the subject to which an image refers. Also, when using a browser, it's what pops up in the little yellow box when you hold your cursor over an image.

AND. The Boolean operator (or connector) that specifies the intersection of sets. When used between words in a search engine query, it specifies that only those records that contain both words are to be retrieved (the words preceding and following the AND). For example, "stomach AND growling" would only retrieve records containing both of those words.

AOL. America Online, the most popular consumer online service.

applet. A small Java-based program used on a Web page to perform certain display, computational, or other functions. The term originates from the idea of "small applications programs."

bookmark. A feature found in Web browsers, analogous to bookmarks used in a book, that remembers the location of a particular Web page and adds it to a list so the page can be returned to easily. Netscape refers to these as "bookmarks," while Internet Explorer uses the term "favorites."

Boolean. Mathematical system of notation created by nineteenth century mathematician George Boole that symbolically represents a relationship between sets (entities). For information retrieval, it uses AND, OR, and NOT (or their equivalents) to identify those records that meet the criteria of having both of two terms within the same record (AND), having either of two terms within the records (OR), or eliminating records that contain a particular term (NOT).

browser. Software that enables display of Web pages by interpreting HTML code, translating it, and performing related tasks. The first widely used browser was Mosaic, which evolved into Netscape. Internet Explorer is the browser developed by Microsoft.

case sensitivity. The ability to recognize the difference between upper and lower case. In information retrieval, it means the difference between possibly being able to recognize White as a name versus white as a color, or AIDS as the disease versus aids as something that provides assistance.

channels. Term used by some online services to organize their services, functions, and Web pages by subject area.

classification. Arrangement of Web sites by subject area, often using a hierarchical scheme with several levels of categories and subcategories.

co-occurrence. Occurrence of two or more specific terms within the same record. Analyzing the frequency of co-occurrence is one technique used to find records that are similar to a selected record.

concept-based retrieval. Retrieval based on finding records that contain words related to the concept searched for, not necessarily the specific word(s) searched for.

crawler. See "spider."

diacritical marks. Marks such as accents that are applied to a letter to indicate a different phonetic value.

directory (Web). Collection of Web page records classified by subject to enable easy browsing of the collection.

domain name. The part of a URL (Web address) that specifies the organization responsible for the Web page. Domain names always have at least two parts: the first part usually identifies the sponsoring organization (for instance, "microsoft"); the second part usually identifies the type of sponsor (for instance, ".com" for "commercial," ".edu" for "educational," etc.).

field. A specific portion of a record, or Web page, such as title, metatags, URL, etc.

file extension. In a file name, such as letter.doc or house.gif, the part of the name that follows the period, usually indicating the type of file.

HTML (HyperText Markup Language). The coding language used to create Web pages, HTML tells a browser how to display a record, including specifications for such things as font, colors, location of images, identification of hypertext links, etc.

home page. The main page of a Web site. Also, the page designated by a user as the page that should be automatically brought up when the user's browser is loaded.

Java. A programming language designed for use on networks, particularly the Internet, which allows programs to be downloaded and run on a variety of platforms. JAVA is incorporated into Web pages with small applications programs called "applets" that provide features such as animation, calculators, games, etc.

JavaScript. A computer language used to write "scripts" for use in browsers to allow creation of such features as scrolling marquees, etc.

meta-search engines. Search services that search several individual search engines and then combine the results.

metatags. The portion (field) of the HTML coding for a Web page that allows the person creating the page to enter text describing the content of the page. The content of metatags is not shown on the page itself when the page is viewed in a browser window.

NEAR. A proximity connector that is used between two words to specify that a document (i.e., a Web page) should be retrieved only when those words are near one another in the document.

nesting. The use of parentheses to specify the way in which terms in a Boolean expression should be grouped—i.e., the order of the operations.

NOT. The Boolean operator (connector) that, when used with a term, eliminates the records containing that term.

OR. The Boolean operator (connector) that, when used between two terms, retrieves all records that contain either term.

portal (Web portal). Web services that position themselves as primary gateways for people to enter the Web, starting points for getting what one needs from the Web. In doing so, these services usually provide a variety of features to attract users to their sites—including search engines, directories, free email, chat rooms, etc.

precision. In information retrieval, the degree to which a group of retrieved records actually match the searcher's needs. More technically, precision is the ratio of the number of relevant items retrieved to the total number of items retrieved (multiplied by 100 percent in order to express the ratio as a percentage). For example, if a query produced 10 records and 6 of them were judged relevant, the precision would be 60 percent. This is sometimes referred to as "relevance."

proximity. The nearness of two terms. Some search engines provide proximity operators, such as NEAR, which allow a user to specify how close two terms must be in order for a record containing those terms to be retrieved.

ranking. The process by which the display/output order of retrieved records is determined. Search engines use algorithms that evaluate records in order to assign a "score" to records, which is meant to be indicative of the relative "relevance" of each record. The retrieved records can then be ranked and listed on the basis of these scores.

recall. In information retrieval, the degree to which a search has actually managed to find all the relevant records in the database. More technically, it is the ratio of the number of relevant records that were retrieved to the total number of relevant records in the database (multiplied by 100 percent in order to express the ratio as a percentage). For example, if a query retrieved 4 relevant records, but there were 10 relevant records in the database, the recall for that search would be 40 percent. Recall is usually difficult to measure since the number of relevant records in a database is often very difficult to determine.

record. A unit of information in a database that contains items of related data. In an address book database, for example, each single record might be the collection of information about one individual person, such as name, address, zip code, phone, etc. In the databases of Web search engines, each record is the collection of information that describes a single Web page.

relevance. The degree to which a record matches the user's query (or the user's needs as expressed in a query). Search engines often assign relevance "scores" to each retrieved record, with the scores representing an estimate of the relevance of that record.

search engines. Programs that accept a user's query, search a database, and return to the user those records that match the query. The term is often used more broadly to refer not just to the information retrieval program itself, but also to the interface and associated features, programs and services.

spider. Programs that search the World Wide Web in order to identify new (or changed) pages for the purpose of adding those pages to a search service's database.

submitted URLs. URLs (Internet addresses) that a person directly submits to a search engine service in order to have that address and its associated Web page added to the service's database.

stop words. Small or frequently occurring words that an information retrieval program does not bother to index (ostensibly because the words are "insignificant," but more likely because the indexing of those words would take up too much storage space or require too much processing).

syntax. The specific order of elements, notations, etc., by which instructions must be submitted to a computer search system.

thesaurus. A listing of terms usually showing the relationship between terms, such as whether one term is narrower or broader than another. Thesauri are used in information retrieval to identify related terms to be searched.

time-out. The amount of time a system will work on a task, or wait for results, before ceasing the task. Also referred to as "waiting time."

truncation. Feature in information retrieval systems that allows one to search using the stem or root of a word and automatically retrieve records with all terms that begin with that string of characters. Truncation is usually specified using a symbol such as an asterisk. For example, in some Web search engines, *town** would retrieve *town, towns, township,* etc.

URL. "Uniform Resource Locator"—the address by which a Web page can be located on the World Wide Web. URLs consist of several parts separated by periods and sometimes slashes.

Usenet. The world's largest system of Internet discussion groups (newsgroups).

waiting time. See "time-out."

Index for The Extreme Searcher's Guide to Web Search Engines

f = figure
t = table

SYMBOLS

A

THE AUTHOR

Randolph E. Hock, Ph.D.

Ran Hock is the principal of Online Strategies, which specializes in creating and delivering customized courses that enable researchers to use the Web effectively. Ran's courses have been delivered to large and small corporations, consulting firms, universities, and associations.

Ran has been a chemistry teacher, a chemistry librarian (at MIT), and the first Data Services Librarian at the University of Pennsylvania. For many years he held training and management positions with DIALOG Information Services and Knight-Ridder Information. He lives in Vienna, Virginia, with his wife and two young children and hopes to someday have time to again pursue his hobby of genealogy.

More CyberAge Books from Information Today, Inc.

Super Searchers Do Business:
The Online Secrets of Top Business Researchers

By Mary Ellen Bates • Edited by Reva Basch

Super Searchers Do Business probes the minds of eleven leading researchers who use the Internet and online services to find critical business information. Through her in-depth interviews, Mary Ellen Bates—a business super searcher herself—gets the pros to reveal how they choose online sources, evaluate search results, and tackle the most challenging business research projects. Loaded with expert tips, techniques and strategies, *Super Searchers Do Business* is the first in the exciting new "Super Searchers" series—and a must-read for anyone who does business research online.

1999 • softbound • ISBN 0-910965-33-1 • $24.95

Great Scouts! CyberGuides for Subject Searching on the Web

By Nora Paul and Margot Williams

Yahoo! was the genesis, the beginning of a noble attempt to organize the unruly Web. Years later, Yahoo! is still the beginning point for many Web users. But as the Web has grown in size, scope, and diversity, Yahoo!'s attempt to be all things to all subjects is often not enough. This guide discusses the growth of Web-based resources, provides guidelines to evaluating resources in specific subject areas, and gives users of subject-specific resources the best alternatives—carefully selected by Nora Paul (The Poynter Institute) and Margot Williams *(The Washington Post)*.

1999 • softbound • ISBN 0-910965-27-7 • $24.95

Internet Blue Pages, 1999 Edition:
The Guide to Federal Government Web Sites

Compiled by Laurie Andriot

With over 900 Web addresses, this guide is designed to help you find any agency easily. Arranged in accordance with the US Government Manual, each entry includes the name of the agency, the Web address (URL), a brief description of the agency, and links to the agency's or subagency's home page. For helpful cross referencing, an alphabetical agency listing and a comprehensive index for subject searching are also included. Regularly updated information and links are provided on the author's Web site.

264 pp. • softbound • ISBN 0-910965-29-3 • $34.95

Finding Statistics Online:
How to Locate the Elusive Numbers You Need

By Paula Berinstein

Need statistics? Find them more quickly and easily than ever—online! Finding good statistics is a challenge for even the most experienced researcher. Today, it's likely that the statistics you need are available online—but where? This book explains how to effectively use the Internet and professional online systems to find the statistics you need to succeed.

320 pp. • softbound • 0-910965-25-0 • $29.95